THE SOCIETY OF PUBLICATION DESIGNERS

TWENTY-SECOND
PUBLICATION
DESIGN
ANNUAL

ACKNOWLEDGMENTS

TWENTY-SECOND
PUBLICATION
DESIGN ANNUAL

DESIGNERS:
Anthony Russell
Samuel Kuo
Anthony Russell, Inc.
New York, NY

ILLUSTRATOR, COVER
AND TITLE PAGES:
Philippe Weisbecker

TYPOGRAPHER:
Typo-Grafix, Inc.
New York, NY

COMPETITION
CHAIRPERSONS:
Nancy Butkus
Amy Bogert

COMPETITION
COMMITTEE:
Jean Chambers
Phyllis Richmond Cox
Virginia Smith

EXHIBITION
COMMITTEE:
Phyllis Richmond Cox
Robert Altemus

CALL FOR ENTRIES
ILLUSTRATOR:
Steve Rydberg

SPECIAL THANKS TO:
Madison Square Press, Inc.
New York, NY

Westvaco Corporation
New York, NY

Monroe Litho, Inc.
Rochester, NY

Anagraphics, Inc.
New York, NY

Stevenson, Inc.
Alexandria, VA

Rudy Baumohl
Felecia Ham
Typo-Grafix, Inc.
New York, NY

Teresa L. Ridley

Dan Baxter
Dana Howell
Allison McGuffin
Susan Weiss

OFFICERS 1986–1987
President:
Melissa Tardiff
Town & Country

Vice President:
Diana LaGuardia
*The New York Times
Magazine*

Vice President:
David Amario
Consumer Electronics

Secretary:
Amy Bogert
American Bookseller

Treasurer:
Lee Ann Jaffee
Lee Ann Jaffee Design

BOARD OF DIRECTORS:
Robert Altemus
Ira Friedman, Inc.

Carla Barr
Connoisseur

Mary K. Baumann
Time-Life Development

Alice Cooke
A to Z Design, Inc.

Nancy Cutler
View Magazine

Phyllis Richmond Cox
Bride's Magazine

John Belkuap
American Lawyer

Virginia Smith
Baruch College

Derek Ungless
Rolling Stone

DIRECTOR:
Bride M. Whelan

DISTRIBUTORS TO THE TRADE
IN THE UNITED STATES AND CANADA:
Watson-Guptill
1515 Broadway
New York, NY 10036

DISTRIBUTORS THROUGHOUT
THE REST OF THE WORLD:
Hearst Publications International
105 Madison Avenue
New York, NY 10016

PUBLISHER:
Madison Square Press, Inc.
10 East 23rd Street
New York, NY 10010

ISBN 0-8230-4887-X

ISSN 0885-6370

PRINTED IN KOREA

2

CONTENTS

The Society of Publication Designers, founded in 1965, is a nonprofit, educational organization dedicated to encouraging, recognizing and recording excellence in editorial design. It serves the special needs of art directors and editorial designers while educating its members and the public about the publication design field.

A variety of activities is offered by the Society to its members. This includes the yearly Competition and the Awards Gala. A monthly Speakers Evening brings together distinguished professionals in the field to share their unique contributions to pub-lication design. *GRIDS*, the monthly news-letter highlighting activities and articles of interest, brings information to members of the goings-on within the publication community. The Portfolio Shows, which showcase new editorial illustrators and photographers, give art directors an oppor-tunity to meet the emerging field of begin-ning professionals, whose work many of them will be using in their individual pub-lications. The Society, more and more, is serving as a forum for the concerns of the editorial design community.

Christopher Austopchuk
Art Director—*CBS Records*

Austopchuk is currently art director of CBS Records and consultant to *Parade Magazine*. He has worked for *Rolling Stone*, Conde Nast and numerous other publications. He has received major design awards from AIGA, the Art Directors Club of New York, Type Directors Club and The Society of Publication Designers. He is an instructor in Graphic and Editorial Design at The School of Visual Arts, New York.

Carla Barr
Creative Director—Vice President, *Calvin Klein Fragrance, Inc.*

Art director of *Connoisseur* from 1983 through February of 1987, Carla has been associate art director of *Life*, *Rolling Stone* and *Esquire*. The recipient of numerous Gold and Silver awards in the SPD Competitions, and a frequent award winner in the New York Art Directors Competition and the AIGA. She is also a lecturer at SVA in New York and the Art Center College of Design in Pasadena, California.

Bob Ciano
Art Director—*Travel & Leisure*

Bob Ciano, former art director of *Life*, is currently the art director of American Express' *Travel & Leisure*. His career has included directorial work at *Esquire*, *The New York Times*, *Opera News* and *CTI Records*. Ciano's work has won countless awards for design, and is a force in the field of publication design.

Stephen Doyle
Principal—*Drenttel, Doyle Partners*

Stephen Doyle has been designing for nine years without knowing the real history of the Garamond family. After three years at *Esquire* under the tutelage of Milton Glaser and then Robert Priest, he worked at *Rolling Stone* before moving on to become art director at M&Co. His current projects range from the feisty *SPY* to *New Republic*, book designs and record covers.

Rip Georges
Art Director—*Regardies*

Rip Georges is currently art director of *Regardies* in Washington, D.C. He joined *West* in 1977, going on to art direct *Revue, Arts & Architecture* and *L.A. Style* before moving East to *Regardies*. Rip has won Gold awards from the Society and awards from the Typographic Institute of America, the Western Publishing Association and the Art Directors Club of L.A.

Laurie Kratochvil
Photography Editor—*Rolling Stone*

Laurie joined *Rolling Stone* as photography editor in 1979 after working at The *Los Angeles Times* and A&M Records. She left *Rolling Stone* to work as photography editor at *New West* (renamed *California*), and served as consultant to Warner Bros. Pictures, Conde Nast and several design firms. In 1982, she returned to *Rolling Stone* as photography editor, the title she currently holds.

Hans Teensma
Design Director—*New England Monthly*

Hans Teensma has designed and art directed *Outside* in San Francisco and *Rolling Stone* in New York, and originated the design of the award-winning *Rocky Mountain* in Denver. In 1983, he moved to Massachusetts to redesign *New Age Journal* before joining *New England Monthly* as its first art director.

Nancy Butkus
Principal—*Nancy Butkus Design*
Chairperson—*22nd Publication Design Annual*

Former art director of *Manhattan, inc.*, Nancy is currently principal of Nancy Butkus Design, for which recently she has redesigned *Cable Guide* and *Ms. Magazine*, among other publication projects.

Deborah Feingold

Amy Bogert
Art Director—*Ms. Magazine*
Chairperson—*22nd Publication Design Annual*

Amy is the art director of *Ms. Magazine*. She art directed American Bookseller for many years, and has held elective office on the SPD board since 1982. She is also a professional illustrator, and her work has appeared on numerous book covers for leading publishing houses.

4

Melissa Tardiff, Art Director of *Town & Country* magazine and President of the Society of Publication Designers, 1986–87.

Slim Aarons

Being an art director has always been challenging—and this year, especially so. No doubt, many readers took great interest in the baseball-bat bashing of art director Terry Dale's office by his editor, Bill Regardie. It seems the editor was trying to make a point about missed deadlines. This cavalier approach epitomizes the classic art director–editor conflict. More recently, the spotlight was on *Manhattan, inc.* and the walkout—led by the editor-in-chief and art director—of its topflight editorial team. The chief ingredient here was the all-too-familiar tension between editorial and business viewpoints. But these are only two examples of the wide-ranging problems faced by art directors in this year of unbridled magazine mania.

The year 1987 has also been one of mergers and acquisitions, startups and shutdowns. The tumult has engendered plenty of action in once-tranquil offices, with art directors moving from one hot seat to the next at an unprecedented rate. And the field remains unsettled.

CBS Magazines was split off from the parent company, and in an interesting twist, *Mother Earth News* has gone upscale. Time, Inc., once a sturdy giant, tested and folded four magazines. Nevertheless, there were more than 300 startups this past year, with focuses on kids and parenting leading the pack.

In the midst of upheaval, the Society of Publication Designers continues to support art directors in the magazine industry. This book celebrates the outstanding efforts and achievements of those art directors who have successfully met the demands of the craft. —*Melissa Tardiff*

Will Hopkins is the winner of the 1987 Herb Lubalin Award for Continuing Excellence in the field of publication design.

Brownie Harris

7

Will Hopkins and magazine design are synonymous. His focus for good design is editorial, and this principle has boosted the Will Hopkins Group into the top rank of designers, winning countless awards from the Art Directors Club, The Society of Publication Designers, AIGA and numerous others.

Will Hopkins, founding member of the Will Hopkins Group, gained his early reputation working with Willi Fleckhaus at *TWEN Magazine* in Germany. In 1966 he joined Allan Hurlbutt at *LOOK*, and became its art director in 1967. He remained at *LOOK*, producing the magazine that gave definition to the 60s.

Since 1977, in partnership with Ira Friedlander, the Group has produced startup designs for such publications as *American Health* and *American Photographer*. Their redesigns have included *Sports Afield, Geo, Horizon, Money, Eastern Review, World Tennis* and, most recently, *Food & Wine*. They also serve as art directors for *Mother Earth News*.

Hopkins' philosophy of design is singular...."The important thing to remember is to keep the graphic treatment from interfering with the message. A designer should not be a decorator, but a communicator."

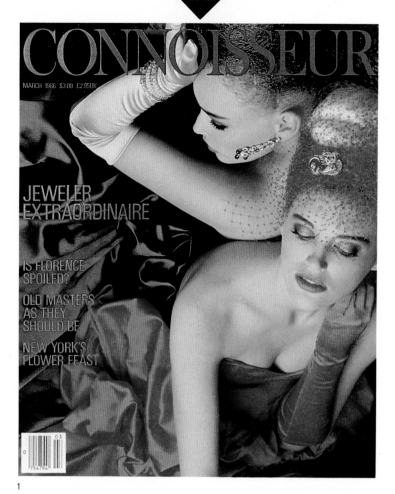

1

10

1
Publication **Connoisseur**
Art Director **Carla Barr**
Designer **Carla Barr**
Photographer **Sandi Fellman**
Publisher **The Hearst Corporation**
Category **Cover**
Date **March 1986**

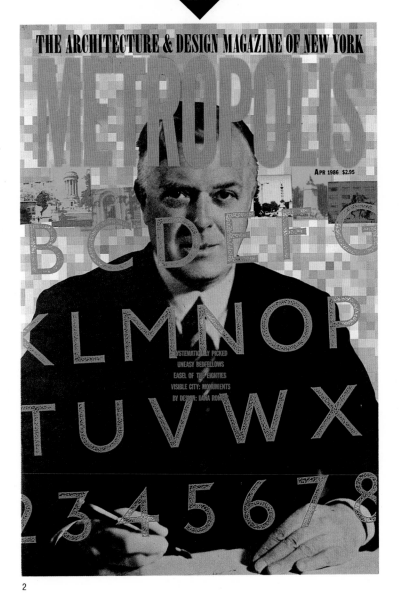

2

2
Publication **Metropolis**
Art Director **Helene Silverman**
Designer **Helene Silverman**
Illustrator **Helene Silverman**
Publisher **Belerophone Publishing, Inc.**
Category **Cover**
Date **April 1986**

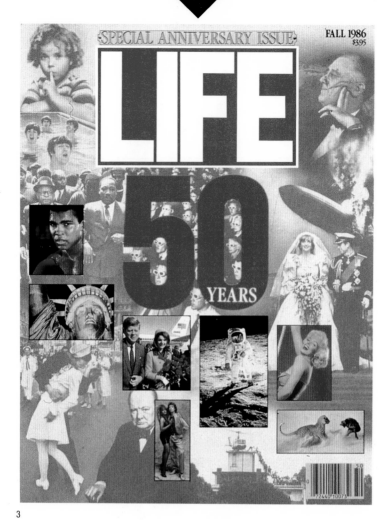

12

3

3
Publication **Life**
Art Director **Charles W. Pates**
Designer **Jean Foos, Keith Davis**
Photographer **Various**
Publisher **Time, Inc.**
Category **Special/Single Issue**
Date **Fall 1986**

3A

3B

3C

3D

3E

13

4A

4B

4C

4

4
Publication **New York**
Art Director **Robert Best**
Designer **Josh Gosfield, David Walters,
Rhonda Rubinstein**
Illustrator **Various**
Photo Editor **Jordan Schaps**
Publisher **Murdoch Magazines, Inc.**
Category **Special/Single Issue**
Date **May 12, 1986**

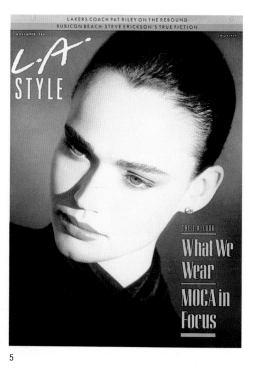

5

5A

15

5B

5
Publication **L.A. Style**
Art Director **Rip Georges**
Publisher **L.A. Style, Inc.**
Category **Overall**
Date **June, November, December 1986**

6

BINGHAMTON

Genus Varium
Hederae

(A Different Breed of Ivy)

University Center at Binghamton
BULLETIN
State University of New York

16

7

6
Publication **Elle**
Art Director **Ron Albrecht**
Publication Director **Regis Pagniez**
Photographer **Gilles Bensimon**
Publisher **Elle Publishing, Inc.**
Category **Cover**
Date **October 1986**

7
Publication **Binghamton Bulletin**
Art Director **Fausto Pellegrini**
Designer **Nadia Pignatone**
Publisher **State University of New York**
Agency **Krukowski Associates**
Category **Cover**
Date **1986**

8

8A

8B

17

8C

8
Publication **Elle**
Art Director **Ron Albrecht**
Publication Director **Regis Pagniez**
Publisher **Elle Publishing, Inc.**
Category **Overall**
Date **May, October, November 1986**

9

9A

9B

9C

9
Publication **Spy**
Art Director **Stephen Doyle**
Designer **Rosemarie Sohmer**
Photographer **George Hein**
Publisher **A/S/M Publications Co.**
Category **Overall**
Date **October, November, December 1986**

18

10

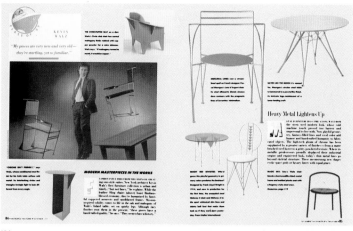

10A

10B

19

10
Publication **Metropolitan Home**
Art Director **Don Morris**
Designer **Richard Ferretti**
Publisher **Meredith Corp.**
Category **Redesign**
Date **November 1986**

11A

20

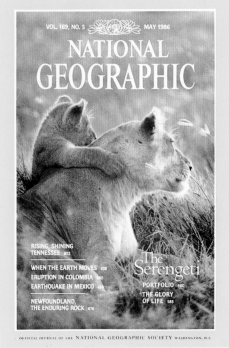

11

11
Publication **National Geographic**
Art Director **Robert W. Madden**
Designer **Robert W. Madden, Gerald A. Valerio,
Constance Phelps**
Photographer **Various**
Publisher **National Geographic Society**
Category **Overall**
Date **December 1986**

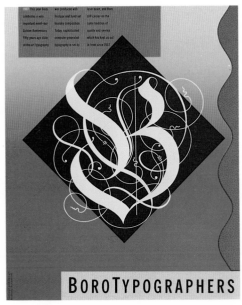

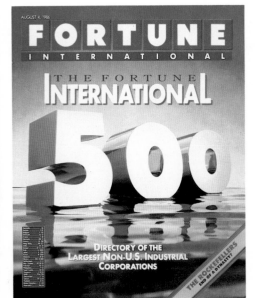

12

14

13

15

12
Publication **Boro Calendar**
Art Director **Anthony Russell**
Designer **Casey Clark**
Publisher **Boro Typographers**
Category **Cover**
Date **November 1986**

14
Publication **Fortune**
Art Director **Margery Peters**
Designer **Margery Peters**
Photographer **Roberto Brosan**
Publisher **Time, Inc.**
Category **Cover**
Date **August 4, 1986**

13
Publication **Normal**
Art Director **Paul Davis**
Designer **Paul Davis**
Illustrator **Paul Davis**
Publisher **Normal Inc.**
Category **Cover**
Date **1986**

15
Publication **M**
Art Director **Owen Hartley**
Designer **Owen Hartley, John Fairchild,**
Michael Coady
Publisher **Fairchild Publications, Inc.**
Category **Cover**
Date **October 1986**

16

18

20

22

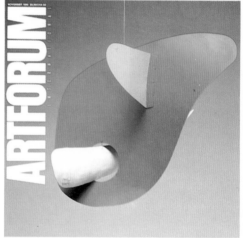

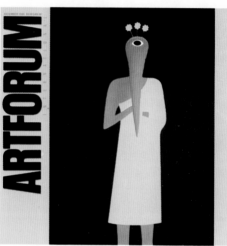

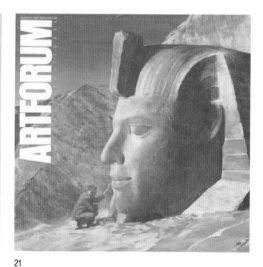

17

19

21

16
Publication **Elle**
Art Director **Ron Albrecht**
Publication Director **Regis Pagniez**
Photographer **Gilles Bensimon**
Publisher **Elle Publishing Inc.**
Category **Cover**
Date **June 1986**

17
Publication **Artforum International**
Art Director **Roger Gorman**
Designer **Frances Reinfeld**
Publisher **Artforum International**
Category **Cover**
Date **November 1986**

18
Publication **Elle**
Art Director **Ron Albrecht**
Publication Director **Regis Pagniez**
Photographer **Gilles Bensimon**
Publisher **Elle Publishing, Inc.**
Category **Cover**
Date **September 1986**

19
Publication **Artforum International**
Art Director **Roger Gorman**
Designer **Frances Reinfeld**
Illustrator **Gino De Dominices**
Publisher **Artforum International**
Category **Cover**
Date **December 1986**

20
Publication **Elle**
Art Director **Phyllis Schefer**
Publication Director **Regis Pagniez**
Photographer **Gilles Bensimon**
Publisher **Elle Publishing, Inc.**
Category **Cover**
Date **December 1986**

21
Publication **Artforum International**
Art Director **Roger Gorman**
Designer **Frances Reinfeld**
Illustrator **Mark Tansey**
Publisher **Artforum International**
Category **Cover**
Date **January 1986**

22

24

26

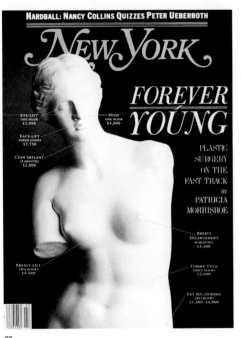

23

25

27

23

28

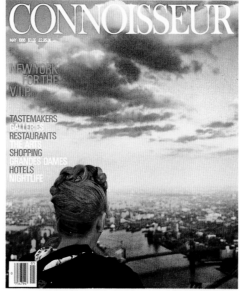

30

32

29

31

33

28
Publication **Connoisseur**
Art Director **Carla Barr**
Designer **Carla Barr**
Photographer **Maggie Steber**
Publisher **The Hearst Corporation**
Category **Cover**
Date **February 1986**

29
Publication **Connoisseur**
Art Director **Carla Barr**
Designer **Carla Barr**
Photographer **Brian Hagiwara**
Publisher **The Hearst Corporation**
Category **Cover**
Date **April 1986**

30
Publication **Connoisseur**
Art Director **Carla Barr**
Designer **Carla Barr**
Photographer **Len Jenshel**
Publisher **The Hearst Corporation**
Category **Cover**
Date **May 1986**

31
Publication **Connoisseur**
Art Director **Carla Barr**
Designer **Carla Barr**
Photographer **Peter Mauss**
Publisher **The Hearst Corporation**
Category **Cover**
Date **November 1986**

32
Publication **Connoisseur**
Art Director **Carla Barr**
Designer **Carla Barr**
Photographer **Peter Menzel**
Publisher **The Hearst Corporation**
Category **Cover**
Date **August 1986**

33
Publication **Connoisseur**
Art Director **Carla Barr**
Designer **Carla Barr**
Photographer **Kenro Izu**
Publisher **The Hearst Corporation**
Category **Cover**
Date **September 1986**

34

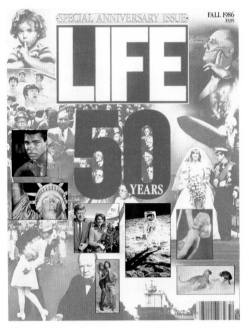

36

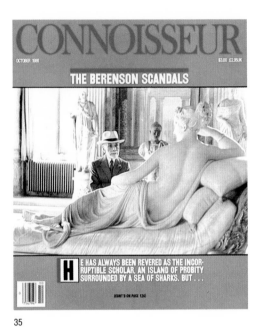

35

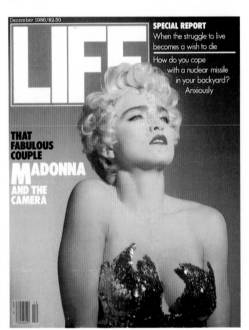

25

37

34
Publication **Connoisseur**
Art Director **Carla Barr**
Designer **Carla Barr**
Photographer **Sandi Fellman**
Publisher **The Hearst Corporation**
Category **Cover**
Date **December 1986**

35
Publication **Connoisseur**
Art Director **Carla Barr**
Designer **Carla Barr**
Photographer **David Seymour/Magnum c. 1955**
Publisher **The Hearst Corporation**
Category **Cover**
Date **October 1986**

36
Publication **Life**
Art Director **Charles W. Pates**
Designer **Charles W. Pates**
Photographer **Various**
Publisher **Time, Inc.**
Category **Cover**
Date **Fall 1986**

37
Publication **Life**
Art Director **Bob Ciano, Robin Brown**
Designer **Robin Brown**
Photographer **Bruce Weber**
Publisher **Time, Inc.**
Category **Cover**
Date **December 1986**

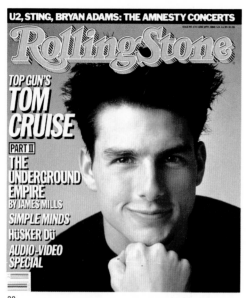

38

39

41

40

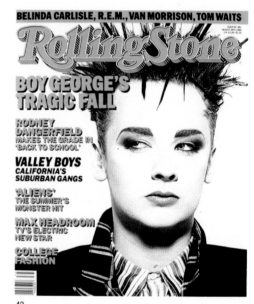

42

39
Publication **Rolling Stone**
Art Director **Derek Ungless**
Designer **Derek Ungless**
Photographer **Matthew Rolston**
Photo Editor **Laurie Kratochvil**
Publisher **Straight Arrow Publishers**
Category **Cover**
Date **June 5, 1986**

41
Publication **Rolling Stone**
Art Director **Derek Ungless**
Designer **Derek Ungless**
Photographer **Bonnie Shiffman**
Publisher **Straight Arrow Publishers**
Category **Cover**
Date **March 27, 1986**

38
Publication **Rolling Stone**
Art Director **Derek Ungless**
Designer **Derek Ungless**
Photographer **Herb Ritts**
Photo Editor **Laurie Kratochvil**
Publisher **Straight Arrow Publishers**
Category **Cover**
Date **June 19, 1986**

40
Publication **Rolling Stone**
Art Director **Derek Ungless**
Designer **Derek Ungless**
Photographer **Matthew Rolston**
Photo Editor **Laurie Kratochvil**
Publisher **Straight Arrow Publishers**
Category **Cover**
Date **October 9, 1986**

42
Publication **Rolling Stone**
Art Director **Derek Ungless**
Designer **Derek Ungless**
Photographer **Norman Watson**
Photo Editor **Laurie Kratochvil**
Publisher **Straight Arrow Publishers**
Category **Cover**
Date **August 28, 1986**

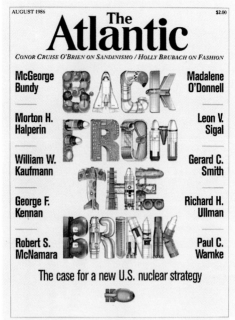

43

45

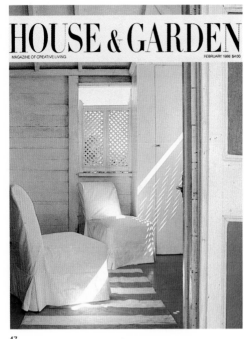

47

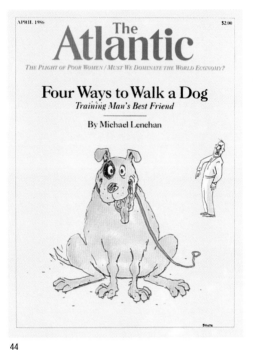

44

46

48

49

50

48
Publication **Spy**
Art Director **Stephen Doyle**
Designer **Rosemarie Sohmer**
Photographer **George Lange**
Publisher **A/S/M Publications Co.**
Category **Cover**
Date **November 1986**

49
Publication **Spy**
Art Director **Stephen Doyle**
Designer **Rosemarie Sohmer**
Photographer **Chris Callis**
Publisher **A/S/M Publications Co.**
Category **Cover**
Date **October 1986**

50
Publication **Spy**
Art Director **Stephen Doyle**
Designer **Rosemarie Sohmer**
Photographer **Bert Stern**
Publisher **A/S/M Publications Co.**
Category **Cover**
Date **December 1986**

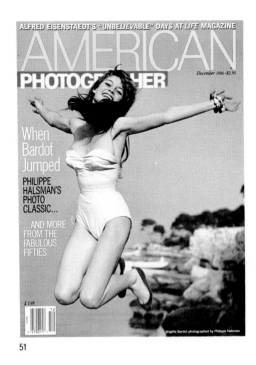

51

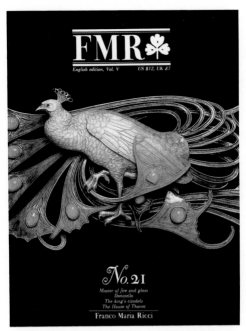

52

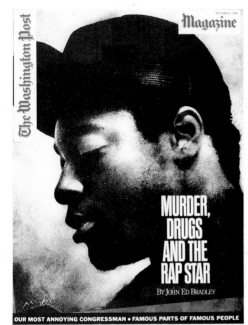

54

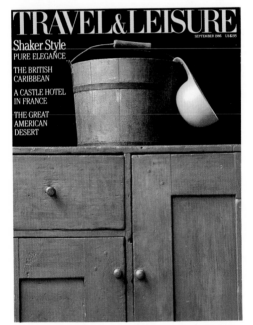

53

52
Publication **FMR**
Art Director **Franco Maria Ricci**
Designer **Laura Casalis**
Category **Cover**
Date **August/September 1986**

51
Publication **American Photographer**
Art Director **Howard Klein**
Designer **Howard Klein**
Photographer **Philippe Halsman**
Publisher **CBS Magazines**
Category **Cover**
Date **December 1986**

53
Publication **Travel & Leisure**
Art Director **Adrian Taylor**
Designer **Adrian Taylor**
Photographer **Michael Melford**
Publisher **American Express Publishing, Co.**
Category **Cover**
Date **September 1986**

54
Publication **Washington Post Magazine**
Art Director **Brian Noyes**
Designer **Jann Alexander**
Photographer **Matt Mahurin**
Publisher **The Washington Post**
Category **Cover**
Date **September 7, 1986**

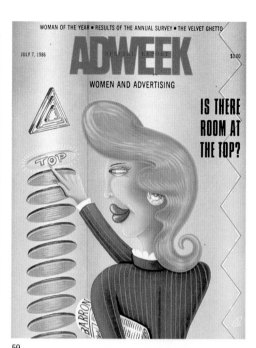

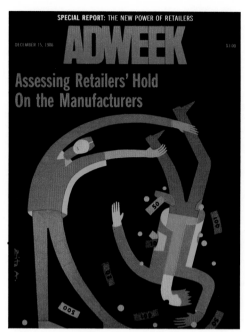

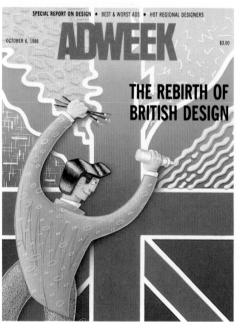

55

57

59

56

58

60

55
Publication **Adweek**
Art Director **Mark Winterford**
Designer **Mark Winterford**
Illustrator **Stephen Turk**
Publisher **A/S/M Communications**
Category **Cover**
Date **August 4, 1986**

56
Publication **Adweek**
Art Director **Mark Winterford**
Designer **Mark Winterford**
Illustrator **Lou Brooks**
Publisher **A/S/M Communications**
Category **Cover**
Date **September 8, 1986**

57
Publication **Adweek**
Art Director **Mark Winterford**
Designer **Mark Winterford**
Illustrator **Zita Asbaghi**
Publisher **A/S/M Communications**
Category **Cover**
Date **December 15, 1986**

58
Publication **Adweek**
Art Director **Mark Winterford**
Designer **Mark Winterford**
Illustrator **Mike Pantuso**
Publisher **A/S/M Communications**
Category **Cover**
Date **October 6, 1986**

59
Publication **Adweek**
Art Director **Mark Winterford**
Designer **Mark Winterford**
Illustrator **Mike Pantuso**
Publisher **A/S/M Communications**
Category **Cover**
Date **July 7, 1986**

60
Publication **Adweek**
Art Director **Mark Winterford**
Designer **Mark Winterford**
Illustrator **Cathleen Toelke**
Publisher **A/S/M Communications**
Category **Cover**
Date **February 25, 1986**

61

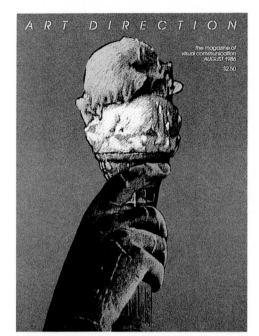

62

63

62
Publication **Art Direction**
Art Director **Carla Block**
Designer **Bob Conge**
Illustrator **Bob Conge**
Publisher **Advertising Trade Publications, Inc.**
Category **Cover**
Date **August 1986**

61
Publication **Adweek**
Art Director **Mark Winterford**
Designer **Mark Winterford**
Illustrator **Javier Romero**
Publisher **A/S/M Communications**
Category **Cover**
Date **April 7, 1986**

63
Publication **American Craft**
Art Director **Kiyoshi Kanai**
Designer **Andrea Wollensak**
Photographer **Dan Cornish/ESTO**
Publisher **American Craft Council**
Category **Cover**
Date **June/July 1986**

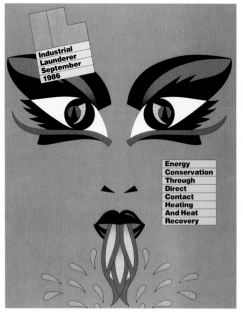

64

66

68

65

67

69

64
Publication **Industrial Launderer**
Art Director **Jack Lefkowitz**
Designer **Jack Lefkowitz**
Illustrator **Virginia Strnad**
Publisher **The Institute of Industrial Launderers**
Category **Cover**
Date **July 1986**

65
Publication **Industrial Launderer**
Art Director **Jack Lefkowitz**
Designer **Jack Lefkowitz**
Illustrator **Virginia Strnad**
Publisher **The Institute of Industrial Launderers**
Category **Cover**
Date **November 1986**

66
Publication **Industrial Launderer**
Art Director **Jack Lefkowitz**
Designer **Jack Lefkowitz**
Illustrator **Virginia Strnad**
Publisher **The Institute of Industrial Launderers**
Category **Cover**
Date **May 1986**

67
Publication **Industrial Launderer**
Art Director **Jack Lefkowitz**
Designer **Jack Lefkowitz**
Illustrator **Virginia Strnad**
Publisher **The Institute of Industrial Launderers**
Category **Cover**
Date **September 1986**

68
Publication **Industrial Launderer**
Art Director **Jack Lefkowitz**
Designer **Jack Lefkowitz**
Illustrator **Virginia Strnad**
Publisher **The Institute of Industrial Launderers**
Category **Cover**
Date **August 1986**

69
Publication **Industrial Launderer**
Art Director **Jack Lefkowitz**
Designer **Jack Lefkowitz**
Illustrator **Virginia Strnad**
Publisher **The Institute of Industrial Launderers**
Category **Cover**
Date **May 1986**

70

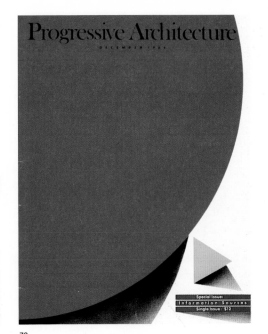

72

71

73

70
Publication **I.D. Magazine**
Design Director **Ann Lee Polus**
Art Director **Clive Jacobson**
Designer **Clive Jacobson**
Publisher **Randolph McAusland**
Category **Cover**
Date **September/October 1986**

71
Publication **I.D. Magazine**
Design Director **Ann Lee Polus**
Art Director **Clive Jacobson**
Designer **Clive Jacobson**
Photographer **Digital Productions**
Publisher **Randolph McAusland**
Category **Cover**
Date **March/April 1986**

72
Publication **Progressive Architecture**
Art Director **Richelle J. Huff**
Designer **Richelle J. Huff**
Publisher **Penton Publishing Co.**
Category **Cover**
Date **December 1986**

73
Publication **Progressive Architecture**
Art Director **Richelle J. Huff**
Designer **Richelle J. Huff**
Photographer **Toshiharu Kitajima**
Publisher **Penton Publishing Co.**
Category **Cover**
Date **April 1986**

74

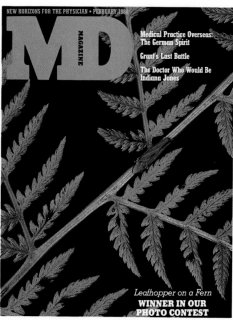

76

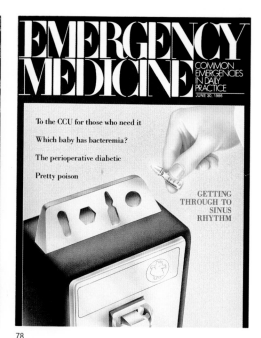

78

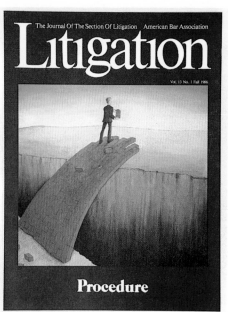

75

77

79

74
Publication **Litigation**
Art Director **Michael Waitsman, Liane Sebastian**
Designer **Michael Waitsman, Liane Sebastian,**
Nathaniel Ascher Marks
Illustrator **W.B. Parks**
Publisher **American Bar Association**
Category **Cover**
Date **Spring 1986**

75
Publication **Litigation**
Art Director **Michael Waitsman, Liane Sebastian**
Designer **Michael Waitsman, Liane Sebastian,**
Nathaniel Ascher Marks
Illustrator **W.B. Parks**
Publisher **American Bar Association**
Category **Cover**
Date **Fall 1986**

76
Publication **MD Magazine**
Art Director **Al Foti, Merrill Cason**
Designer **Merrill Cason**
Photographer **K.A. Deitcher**
Publisher **MD Publications**
Category **Cover**
Date **February 1986**

77
Publication **MD Magazine**
Art Director **Mitch Shannon**
Designer **Mitch Shannon**
Illustrator **Bernard Durin**
Publisher **MD Publications**
Category **Cover**
Date **May 1986**

78
Publication **Emergency Medicine**
Art Director **Lois Erlacher**
Designer **Lois Erlacher**
Illustrator **Alan Wallerstein**
Publisher **Emergency Medicine Magazine**
Category **Cover**
Date **June 30, 1986**

79
Publication **Chief Fire Executive**
Art Director **Karen Lehrer**
Designer **Karen Lehrer**
Photographer **S. Baker Vail**
Publisher **Firehouse Communications Co.**
Category **Cover**
Date **October/November 1986**

80

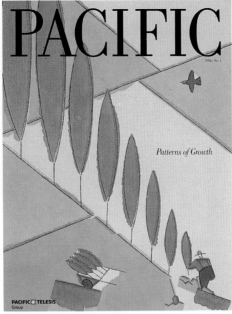

82

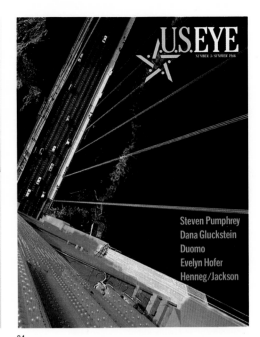

84

81

83

85

80
Publication **The Clarion**
Art Director **Faye H. Eng, Anthony T. Yee**
Designer **Faye H. Eng, Anthony T. Yee**
Photographer **Carleton Palmer**
Publisher **The Clarion, Inc.**
Category **Cover**
Date **Winter 1986**

81
Publication **The Clarion**
Art Director **Faye H. Eng, Anthony T. Yee**
Designer **Faye H. Eng, Anthony T. Yee**
Publisher **The Clarion, Inc.**
Category **Cover**
Date **Fall 1986**

82
Publication **Pacific**
Art Director **Michael Mabry**
Designer **Michael Mabry, Peter Soe, Jr.**
Illustrator **Philippe Weisbecker**
Publisher **Pacific Telesis Co.**
Category **Cover**
Date **March 1986**

83
Publication **Pacific**
Art Director **Michael Mabry**
Designer **Michael Mabry, Renee Holsen**
Illustrator **John Hersey**
Publisher **Pacific Telesis Co.**
Category **Cover**
Date **December 1986**

84
Publication **US Eye**
Art Director **Anthony Russell**
Designer **Casey Clark**
Photographer **Charles Jackson, Robert Henneg**
Publisher **US Eye Publishing**
Category **Cover**
Date **August 1986**

85
Publication **RP Magazine**
Art Director **Douglas Wolfe**
Designer **John Howze**
Illustrator **Jim Buckels**
Publisher **Ralston Purina Co.**
Category **Cover**
Date **#1 in 1986**

IN FOCUS: Cable—Who's Got the Clout

CHANNELS

$2.95   OF COMMUNICATIONS   MARCH 1986

Going Fourth
On the morning of September 4, 1985, Rupert Murdoch stood in a room full of immigrants and swore a solemn oath renouncing all allegiance to foreign princes. And so Murdoch, and his accountants and his lawyers and his bankers, his vicar Barry Diller, and his mighty world-wide cash flow, laid siege to that grim fortress, the three-net-

86

Is TCI Cable's Bully?

CHANNELS

$2.95   THE BUSINESS OF COMMUNICATIONS   OCTOBER 1986

The Class of '86

Channels' yearly Salute to Excellence includes a funny guy and his writers, plus six other better-dressed paragons of originality, guts and all-around niftiness.

The Letterman Gang

87

FOCUS: British TV's Nervous System

CHANNELS

$2.95   OF COMMUNICATIONS   AUGUST 1986

John Sias, executive clown, just got serious.

He and his Cap Cities bosses discovered ABC was not the company they thought they'd bought. Now they mean to run it as no network has ever been run before.

88

36

86
Publication **Channels**
Art Director **Marian Chin**
Designer **Walter Bernard, Milton Glaser**
Photographer **Reuters-Bettman News Photos**
Publisher **CC Publishing, Inc.**
Category **Cover**
Date **March 1986**

87
Publication **Channels**
Art Director **Carol Layton**
Designer **Walter Bernard, Milton Glaser**
Photographer **Carl Fischer**
Publisher **CC Publishing, Inc.**
Category **Cover**
Date **October 1986**

88
Publication **Channels**
Art Director **Marian Chin**
Designer **Walter Bernard, Milton Glaser**
Photographer **Bill Kobasz**
Publisher **CC Publishing, Inc.**
Category **Cover**
Date **August 1986**

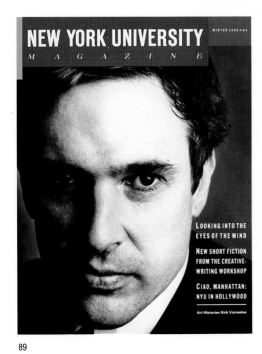

89

90

92

91

90
Publication **Scholastic Action**
Art Director **Lisa Francella**
Designer **Vivian Ng**
Illustrator **Bill Kobasz**
Photographer **Phil Stern/Globe**
Publisher **Scholastic, Inc.**
Category **Cover**
Date **January 31, 1986**

89
Publication **New York University Magazine**
Art Director **Steven Hoffman**
Designer **Steven Hoffman**
Photographer **Timothy Greenfield Sanders**
Publisher **New York University**
Category **Cover**
Date **Winter 1986**

91
Publication **World**
Art Director **Anthony Russell**
Designer **Jan McNeil**
Illustrator **David Lesh**
Publisher **Peat Marwick**
Category **Cover**
Date **April 1986**

92
Publication **Common Cause**
Art Director **Jeffrey L. Dever/Dever Designs**
Designer **Jeffrey L. Dever/Dever Designs**
Photographer **Jerry Mesmer/Adams Studio Inc.**
Publisher **Common Cause**
Category **Cover**
Date **November/December 1986**

93

95

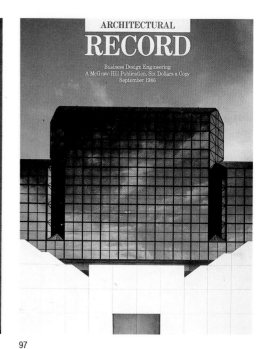

97

94

96

93
Publication **Architectural Record**
Art Director **Alex Stillano**
Designer **Anna Egger-Schlesinger**
Publisher **McGraw-Hill Publications Co.**
Category **Cover**
Date **January 1986**

95
Publication **Architectural Record**
Art Director **Alex Stillano**
Designer **Anna Egger-Schlesinger**
Publisher **McGraw-Hill Publications Co.**
Category **Cover**
Date **May 1986**

94
Publication **Architectural Record**
Art Director **Alex Stillano**
Designer **Alberto Bucchianeri**
Publisher **McGraw-Hill Publications Co.**
Category **Cover**
Date **Mid-September 1986**

96
Publication **Architectural Record**
Art Director **Alex Stillano**
Designer **Alberto Bucchianeri**
Publisher **McGraw-Hill Publications Co.**
Category **Cover**
Date **October 1986**

97
Publication **Architectural Record**
Art Director **Alex Stillano**
Designer **Alex Stillano**
Publisher **McGraw-Hill Publications Co.**
Category **Cover**
Date **September 1986**

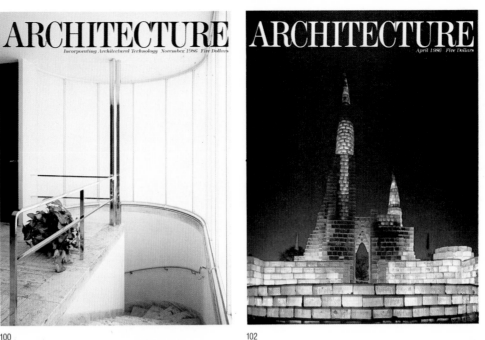

98

99

101

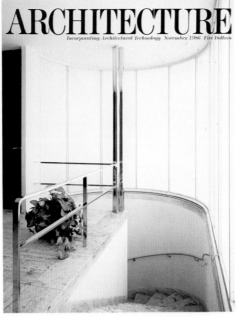

100

102

98
Publication **Architecture**
Art Director **Carole J. Palmer**
Photographer **Roy Flamm**
Publisher **The American Institute of Architecture**
Category **Cover**
Date **February 1986**

99
Publication **Architecture Minnesota**
Art Director **Jim Cordaro**
Designer **Jim Cordaro**
Photographer **George Heinrich**
Publisher **Minnesota Society, The American**
Institute of Architecture
Category **Cover**
Date **November-December 1986**

100
Publication **Architecture**
Art Director **Carole J. Palmer**
Photographer **Pavel Stecha**
Publisher **The American Institute of Architecture**
Category **Cover**
Date **November 1986**

101
Publication **Architecture Minnesota**
Art Director **Jim Cordaro**
Designer **Jim Cordaro**
Photographer **Lea Babcock**
Publisher **Minnesota Society, The American**
Institute of Architecture
Category **Cover**
Date **January-February 1986**

102
Publication **Architecture**
Art Director **Carole J. Palmer**
Photographer **George Heinrich**
Publisher **The American Institute of Architecture**
Category **Cover**
Date **April 1986**

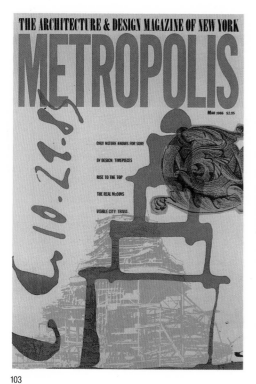

103

104

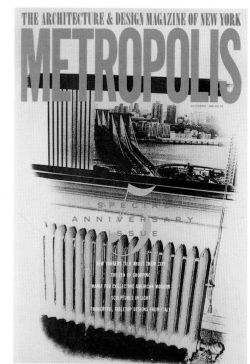

105

103
Publication **Metropolis**
Art Director **Helene Silverman**
Designer **Helene Silverman**
Publisher **Belerophon**
Category **Cover**
Date **March 1986**

104
Publication **Metropolis**
Art Director **Helene Silverman**
Designer **Helene Silverman**
Photographer **Ken Collins**
Publisher **Belerophon**
Category **Cover**
Date **December 1986**

105
Publication **Metropolis**
Art Director **Helene Silverman**
Designer **Helene Silverman**
Photographer **Elaine Ellman**
Publisher **Belerophon**
Category **Cover**
Date **October 1986**

106

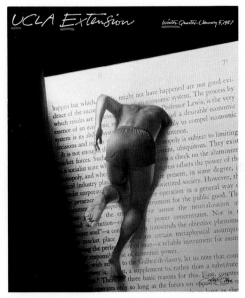

107

109

108

107
Publication **UCLA Extension**
Art Director **Saul Bass, Art Goodman**
Designer **Saul Bass**
Photographer **George Arakaki**
Publisher **University of California at Los Angeles**
Category **Cover**
Date **December 1986**

106
Publication **Step-By-Step Graphics**
Art Director **Mike Hammer**
Designer **Greg Paul**
Illustrator **Wilson McLean**
Publisher **Dynamic Graphics, Inc.**
Agency **Brady-Paul, Inc.**
Category **Cover**
Date **July/August 1986**

108
Publication **Outside Business**
Art Director **Ken Ovryn**
Designer **Ken Ovryn**
Illustrator **John Youssi**
Publisher **Outside Magazine**
Category **Cover**
Date **May/June 1986**

109
Publication **Family Therapy Networker**
Art Director **Bevi Chagnon/Artlandish!**
Designer **Bevi Chagnon**
Illustrator **Marla Tarbox**
Publisher **The Family Therapy Networker**
Category **Cover**
Date **November 1986**

110

112

111

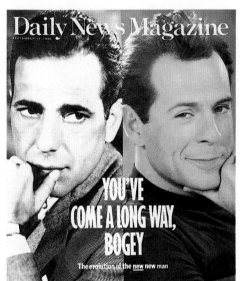

113

110
Publication **American Craft**
Art Director **Kiyoshi Kanai**
Designer **Andrea Wollensak**
Photographer **Bruce Miller**
Publisher **American Craft Council**
Category **Cover**
Date **April/May 1986**

111
Publication **W**
Art Director **Owen Hartley**
Designer **Owen Hartley**
Photographer **Patrick McCarthy**
Publisher **Fairchild Publications**
Category **Cover**
Date **September 22, 1986**

112
Publication **The NFL and You**
Art Director **Glen Iwasaki**
Photographer **Ed Ikuta**
Publisher **National Football League**
Category **Cover**
Date **1986–87**

113
Publication **Daily News Magazine**
Art Director **Janet Froelich**
Designer **Janet Froelich**
Publisher **The Tribune Co.**
Category **Cover**
Date **September 14, 1986**

114

116

115

117

114
Publication **The Plain Dealer Magazine**
Art Director **Gerard Sealy**
Designer **Gerard Sealy**
Illustrator **Patrick Blackwell**
Publisher **Plain Dealer Publishing Co.**
Category **Cover**
Date **September 28, 1986**

115
Publication **The Plain Dealer Magazine**
Art Director **Gerard Sealy**
Designer **Gerard Sealy**
Illustrator **Merle Nacht**
Publisher **Plain Dealer Publishing Co.**
Category **Cover**
Date **December 14, 1986**

116
Publication **Florida Magazine**
Art Director **Santa Choplin**
Designer **Santa Choplin**
Illustrator **Buddy Hickerson**
Publisher **Sentinel Communications Co.**
Category **Cover**
Date **December 7, 1986**

117
Publication **Math**
Art Director **Joan Michael**
Designer **Scott Frommer**
Illustrator **Ron Zalme**
Publisher **Scholastic, Inc.**
Category **Cover**
Date **November 1986**

118

120

122

119

121

123

118
Publication **The New York Times Magazine**
Art Director **Ken Kendrick, Diana LaGuardia**
Designer **Diana LaGuardia**
Photographer **Michael O'Neill**
Publisher **The New York Times**
Category **Cover**
Date **July 13, 1986**

119
Publication **The New York Times**
Art Director **"Editors and Art Directors of
The New York Times"**
Publisher **The New York Times**
Category **Cover**
Date **January 29, 1986**

120
Publication **The New York Times Magazine**
Art Director **Diana LaGuardia**
Designer **Diana LaGuardia**
Photographer **Ricardo Salas**
Publisher **The New York Times**
Category **Cover**
Date **November 2, 1986**

121
Publication **The New York Times**
Art Director **Nicki Kalish**
Designer **Nicki Kalish**
Illustrator **Edward Gorey**
Publisher **The New York Times**
Category **Cover**
Date **June 4, 1986**

122
Publisher **The New York Times Magazine**
Art Director **Nancy Kent**
Designer **Nancy Kent**
Illustrator **Guy Billout**
Publisher **The New York Times**
Category **Cover**
Date **May 4, 1986**

123
Publication **The New York Times**
Art Director **Linda Brewer**
Designer **Linda Brewer**
Illustrator **Michael Bartolos**
Publisher **The New York Times**
Category **Cover**
Date **December 7, 1986**

124

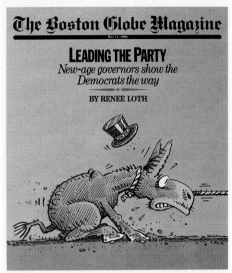

126

128

125

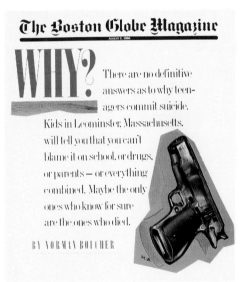

127

129

124
Publication **The Boston Globe Magazine**
Art Director **Lynn Staley**
Designer **Lynn Staley**
Illustrator **Matt Mahurin**
Publisher **The Boston Globe**
Category **Cover**
Date **February 16, 1986**

125
Publication **The Boston Globe Magazine**
Art Director **Lynn Staley**
Designer **Lynn Staley**
Illustrator **Gene Greif**
Publisher **The Boston Globe**
Category **Cover**
Date **July 20, 1986**

126
Publication **The Boston Globe Magazine**
Art Director **Lynn Staley**
Designer **Lynn Staley**
Illustrator **Elwood Smith**
Publisher **The Boston Globe**
Category **Cover**
Date **May 11, 1986**

127
Publication **The Boston Globe Magazine**
Art Director **Lynn Staley**
Designer **Lynn Staley**
Illustrator **Marshall Arisman**
Publisher **The Boston Globe**
Category **Cover**
Date **August 3, 1986**

128
Publication **The Boston Globe Magazine**
Art Director **Lynn Staley**
Designer **Lynn Staley**
Illustrator **Doug Smith**
Publisher **The Boston Globe**
Category **Cover**
Date **May 25, 1986**

129
Publication **The Boston Globe**
Art Director **Lucy Bartholomay**
Designer **Lucy Bartholomay**
Photographer **Michael Weisbrot**
Publisher **The Boston Globe**
Category **Cover**
Date **November 9, 1986**

THE ROLLING STONE INTERVIEW SAM SHEPARD

The theater critic Michael Feingold once remarked that the paradox of Sam Shepard consisted in his having "the mind of a Kafka trapped in the body of a Jimmy Stewart."

It was Franz Kafka who wrote that "a book must be the ax for the frozen sea in us." And in the more than forty plays that Sam Shepard has written since 1964, this American playwright has been breaking open that frozen sea with an originality of vision, a jolting intermingling of humor and grief, a profound examination of the hopes and failures of the American family and an astonishing ear for the cadences of the American idiom. With plays like *The Unseen Hand*, *Curse of the Starving Class*, *Buried Child* (for which he won the 1979 Pulitzer Prize), *True West*, *Fool for Love* and the recent *A Lie of the Mind*, Shepard has cloaked himself in the mantle once worn by Eugene O'Neill and Tennessee Williams.

This Franz Kafka with a lariat, this desert-haunted cowboy-stranger, has also, as an actor, attained the popularity of matinee idols such as Jimmy Stewart and Gary Cooper. With his lean,

BY JONATHAN COTT
PHOTOGRAPHS BY BRUCE WEBER

130

THE ROLLING STONE INTERVIEW JACK NICHOLSON

BY FRED SCHRUERS

Jack Nicholson's Hollywood Hills home perches above an empty ravine – a rare prospect amid these overbuilt hills of dirt and scrub. On the hot afternoon when I arrive, a chain-link fence is being installed (not, I'm later told, at Nicholson's instigation) on the winding driveway he shares with Marlon Brando. Despite the fence and an electronic inspection of visitors, Nicholson's complex – two houses, a row of carports topped by a basketball hoop, and a deck equipped with a pool and a commanding

132

Rodney Dangerfield has wealth, fame, a hit movie and the respect of almost everybody but himself. Life, whew, it's rough. By Lewis Grossberger

RESPECT AT LAST

Hot Rodney!

So now it's Rodney the movie star. Five years ago, last time I talked to him, he was merely America's fastest-rising old comedian. Now he's Rodney, summer-film comet. Every time you turn around, the guy's career goes up a notch.

We're in the back of a chauffeured stretch with all the trimmings. Bar, TV, phone are all ignored. Rodney is spooning up a big bowl of cereal, fruit and skim milk. He's on some kind of diet kick, making a stab at health, not too optimistically. "I got no willpower, forget it, will ya? It's

46
131

TIP O'NEILL'S LAST HURRAH

Tip O'Neill could not have planned a more graceful exit. The elections last month gave his beloved Democratic party a majority in both houses of the Congress. His own seat in the House of Representatives, which he is relinquishing after thirty-four years, passed with his blessing to Joseph P. Kennedy II – the nephew of John F. Kennedy, whom O'Neill succeeded in the seat in 1953. Only five years after the lowest point of his career – when he was openly ridiculed by the Republicans, the press and some members of his own party – the Speaker of the House came down from the Hill to tell the American people, "The Reagan revolution is over."

The rise of Thomas P. O'Neill is a story of the old politics. His grandfather came from County Cork, Ireland, to settle in North Cambridge, Massachusetts, where he found work as a bricklayer. His father started a small contracting business there and was elected to the city council. O'Neill entered the Massachusetts state legislature at the age of twenty-four – and has held public office ever since.

In 1952, JFK ran for the U.S. Senate; a year earlier he had privately

BY WILLIAM GREIDER
PHOTOGRAPH BY NIGEL DICKSON

133

H

BY FRED SCHRUERS

CAN'T STOP THE GIRL

PHOTOGRAPH BY MATTHEW ROLSTON

134

130
Publication **Rolling Stone**
Art Director **Derek Ungless**
Designer **Raul Martinez, Angelo Savaides**
Photographer **Bruce Weber**
Photo Editor **Laurie Kratochvil**
Publisher **Straight Arrow Publishers**
Category **Single Page/Spread**
Date **December 18, 1986**

131
Publication **Rolling Stone**
Art Director **Derek Ungless**
Designer **Raul Martinez**
Photographer **Deborah Feingold**
Photo Editor **Laurie Kratochvil**
Publisher **Straight Arrow Publishers**
Category **Single Page/Spread**
Date **August 28, 1986**

132
Publication **Rolling Stone**
Art Director **Derek Ungless**
Designer **Raul Martinez**
Photographer **Herb Ritts**
Publisher **Straight Arrow Publishers**
Category **Single Page/Spread**
Date **August 14, 1986**

133
Publication **Rolling Stone**
Art Director **Derek Ungless**
Designer **Raul Martinez, Angelo Savaides**
Photographer **Nigel Dickson**
Photo Editor **Laurie Kratochvil**
Publisher **Straight Arrow Publishers**
Category **Single Page/Spread**
Date **December 18, 1986**

134
Publication **Rolling Stone**
Art Director **Derek Ungless**
Designer **Raul Martinez**
Photo Editor **Laurie Kratochvil**
Photographer **Matthew Rolston**
Publisher **Straight Arrow Publishers**
Category **Single Page/Spread**
Date **June 5, 1986**

EVENING BECOMES ELECTRIC

On the centenary of the traditional tux, evening wear goes rock & roll. One hundred years ago, Griswold "Grizzy" Lorillard wore the first tuxedo. Fifty-five years later, Les Paul popped the first solid-body guitar with electricity. Today, conventional black-and-white formal wear is taking on a charge of its own as men and women adapt it to their own styles. And bars, restaurants and the new "floating" clubs (those that share locations with other clubs on different days of the week) provide a wide spectrum of big-city backdrops for well-dressed night players. Here, photographed in New York City and Los Angeles, are musicians and actresses who have developed variations on classic themes that may have Mr. Lorillard rolling over to the tune of "Blue Suede Shoes." **BY LAURIE SCHECHTER**

PHOTOGRAPHS BY MICHAEL O'BRIEN

135

BY JUDITH MILLER AND MARIE COLVIN

QADDAFI ON THE EDGE

Three and a half months after the American air attack on Libya, a shellshocked Colonel Muammar el-Qaddafi appears to be losing control of his country and himself

'He was an agent of the Gestapo, and he caused the death of thousands of Jews. We have a file on this.'

137

THE ROLLING STONE INTERVIEW
BILLY JOEL

The atmosphere at Kaufman Astoria Studios in Queens combines all the giddiness and physical discomfort of a back-to-school shopping spree. Billy Joel has interrupted rehearsals for his first tour in nearly three years to sample the latest fashions for potential stage wear — and he's getting expert advice from his wife, model Christie Brinkley, who is sitting on the floor with their nine-month-old daughter, Alexa Ray.

The short, broad Joel — whom Christie always calls Joe — waddles into the room, decked out in a flashy, double-breasted gray suit. "Do I look like an English rock star?" he queries in a mock-British accent, while bumping and grinding his hips and growling out the riff to Robert Palmer's "I Didn't Mean to Turn You On." Christie, meanwhile, is up on her feet, walking around Billy, examining the look. "When you get that suit made in your size, don't get it made too small," she advises. "And don't do that short-sleeves routine." "Those pants make you look really slim."

BY ANTHONY DeCURTIS   PHOTOGRAPH BY ALBERT WATSON

136

47

135
Publication **Rolling Stone**
Art Director **Derek Ungless**
Designer **Derek Ungless**
Photographer **Michael O'Brien**
Photo Editor **Laurie Kratochvil**
Publisher **Straight Arrow Publishers**
Category **Single Page/Spread**
Date **November 20, 1986**

136
Publication **Rolling Stone**
Art Director **Derek Ungless**
Designer **Raul Martinez**
Photographer **Albert Watson**
Photo Editor **Laurie Kratochvil**
Publisher **Straight Arrow Publishers**
Category **Single Page/Spread**
Date **November 6, 1986**

137
Publication **Rolling Stone**
Art Director **Derek Ungless**
Designer **Angelo Savaides**
Photographer **G. Noel, Le Figaro, Gamma Liason**
Photo Editor **Laurie Kratochvil**
Publisher **Straight Arrow Publishers**
Category **Single Page/Spread**
Date **August 14, 1986**

Modern Romance

By Christina Robb

What is this thing called love? We want it. We need it. We also fear it at times, and we may spend years searching for and avoiding love so rhythmically that our lives become a symphony of frustration.

We have styles of searching for love, styles of finding and being found, and almost any road may lead to love. I always had the most proper introductions to the men I fell for. I knew my husband for three years before we thought about connecting any other way. By contrast, a dear friend of mine met the first love of her life in a city street on a rainy day the asked to share her umbrella! Years later, she sat down next to the second, lasting love of her life for the first time on a city bus. They had their first date a few days later.

My friend's fellow passenger turned out to be separated from a mentally ill wife who played crazy games with him, via lawyer, for several years. And for all those years, my friend begged him to say he'd marry her when the divorce came through. Being a certain kind of man, he refused to promise something he couldn't yet deliver and left my friend in chronic, anxious suspense. On the day his divorce was final, he asked my friend to marry him.

She said no! Suddenly she found herself panicked at the idea of taking such a giant step with one man. She began to question everything about their relationship. He became the partner and she the pursued, and who knows? Maybe they just had to reverse roles long enough for my

friend to get the message that he wanted her as much as she wanted him. They finally eloped, years after they'd met on the bus.

One of the problems with the way social scientists write about love is that they underplay its grounding, centering role in our lives. Often what experts end up writing about is not love but what gets in love's way. Psychologists write about love as infatuation or addiction, as obsession or jealousy. Or they write about the symptoms or tools of love and mistake a part for the whole. Sigmund Freud called love "aim-inhibited sexuality." (In a wiser moment, he got out of love's way and *Continued on page 57*

Illustration by Vivienne Flesher

138

IN AMALFI

On the rocky beach next to the Cobalto, the boys were painting the boats. In June the tourist season would begin, and the rowboats would be launched, most of them rented by the hour to Americans and Swedes and Germans. The Americans would keep them on the water five or 10 minutes longer than the time for which they had been rented. The Swedes, usually thin and always pale, would know they had begun to burn after half an hour and return the boats early. It was difficult to generalize about the Germans. They were often blamed for the beer bottles that washed ashore, although others pointed out that this wasn't likely, because the Germans were such clean, meticulous people. The young German girls had short, spiky hair and wore earrings in shapes it would be difficult to find the right theorem for in a geometry book. The men were more conventional, wearing socks with their sandals, although when they were on the beach they often wore the sandals barefooted and stuffed the socks in their pockets.

What Christine knew about the tourists came from her very inadequate understanding of Italian. This was the second time she had spent a month in Amalfi, and while few of the people were friendly, it was clear that some of them recognized her. The beach boys talked to her about the tourists, as though she did not belong to that category. Two of them (there were usually six to 10 boys at the beach, working on the boats, renting chairs, or throwing a Frisbee) had asked some questions about Andrew. They wanted to know if it was her father who sat upstairs in the bar, at the same table every day, feet resting on the scrollwork of the blue metal railing, writing. Christine said that he was not her father. Then another boy punched his friend and said, "I told you he was her *mari*." She shook her head no. A third boy — probably not much interested in what his friends might find out, anyway — said that his brother-in-law was expanding his business. The brother-in-law was going to rent *Continued on page 31*

Fiction by Ann Beattie

Illustration by Vivienne Flesher

139

PIZZA MAN

Confessions of a half-baked entrepreneur

By Daniel Golden

Jon Fuller and I wouldn't settle for the sweaty, exploitative, minimum-wage jobs that are reserved for high schoolers who don't know any better — pumping gas, pushing supermarket carriages, French-frying fast food. Instead, we fulfilled the American fantasy and became entrepreneurs, chasing success by our wits and our wares, hawking pizzas in college dormitories in our home town of Amherst. And now we had run into trouble at the University of Massachusetts. Not with the undergraduates — they were salivating in that spring of 1974. When they heard us shout, "Hot Bell's pizza here," they rushed into the corridors as if we were giving away free tickets to a Bob Dylan concert.

No, the trouble came from the grad students who stayed in the dorms first in return for protecting undergraduates against interlopers like ourselves. For weeks, we had neutralized them through guilt. Whenever they threatened eviction, we protested that they would bankrupt us, because we had to vape Bell's for any unsold pizzas. If they would just let us finish our rounds today, we promised, we would never return. They always relented. We always returned.

Then one night they ignored our pleas and kicked us out. And if we hadn't stumbled upon a group of pot smokers who had the munchies between about 30 cents and a half-dozen stale pizzas.

The next evening, we consulted Mr. Bell, who listened poker-faced to our plight. Then he rummaged through his papers for a few minutes and retrieved a letter on UMass stationery.

"Wave it in their faces, and you won't have any problems," he said.

If memory serves, the letter read, "Dear Mr.

I said, "Mr. Bell, I don't understand how this letter allows us to sell pizzas in the Sylvan dorms."

"It does if you hold it this way," he responded. He grasped the letter between forefinger and thumb and dangled it aloft. The pertinent part now went, "Dear Mr. Bell: Your solicitors are absolutely THUMB0 permitted under any circumstances to sell pizzas...."

"I'll give it a try," I said. To my amazement, the stratagem worked. Too polite to grab the letter, the graduate students skimmed the uncovered words and *Continued on page 62*

Illustration by Jose Cruz

140

The Real Wheeler-Dealers

By J. Francis Gladstone

REMEMBER *BULLITT* WITH STEVE McQUEEN? And the car chase on the San Francisco switchbacks? Was McQueen the real hero of the film, or was it the Ford Mustang, Lee Iacocca's baby? Celluloid macho man and celluloid machine seemed to be inseparable. Throughout the era of Al Capone, Walter Chrysler's streamlined airflows seemed as natural a mob appendage as did the Tommy guns poking from their windows. Looking back on a more innocent age, it is difficult to separate the image of Harold Lloyd from the image of the Model T he drove around landscapes made lunatic by the car's antics. The movement of cars runs through the silent film era, carrying the comedians on their careening careers.

Today cars are a fact of life. More people in the United States have cars than do people in any other country. Cars pollute the atmosphere, and they kill people — about a quarter of a million worldwide annually. They plug up old cities. They are an endless drain on one's finances, more so than any other consumable. Low them or hate them, cosset them or abuse them, cars have become inseparable from modern living.

Yet only 100 years ago there were very few cars, only about four or five experimental. *Continued on page 66*

Karl Benz, Henry Ford, and other pioneers of the car industry truly made the world go round.

141

48

138
Publication **The Boston Globe**
Art Director **Lynn Staley**
Designer **Lynn Staley**
Illustrator **Vivienne Flesher**
Publisher **The Boston Globe**
Category **Single Page/Spread**
Date **February 9, 1986**

139
Publication **The Boston Globe**
Art Director **Lynn Staley**
Designer **Lynn Staley**
Illustrator **Vivienne Flesher**
Publisher **The Boston Globe**
Category **Single Page/Spread**
Date **September 28, 1986**

140
Publication **The Boston Globe**
Art Director **Lynn Staley**
Designer **Lynn Staley**
Illustrator **Jose Cruz**
Publisher **The Boston Globe**
Category **Single Page/Spread**
Date **June 8, 1986**

141
Publication **The Boston Globe**
Art Director **Lynn Staley**
Designer **Gail Anderson**
Illustrator **Archives**
Publisher **The Boston Globe**
Category **Single Page/Spread**
Date **August 24, 1986**

Part magic, part comedy, part circus act: *Penn & Teller* is hard to define, but at the very least it's brilliant

WHAT YOU SEE, WHAT YOU GET

By Kevin Kelly

Estragon: "You don't have to look."
Vladimir: "You can't help looking."
— Waiting for Godot

"Because it's here but it isn't."
— Penn & Teller

At a recent performance of *Penn & Teller*, the small-scale off-Broadway "magic show" that plights the troth that feeds it, a young member of the audience who gave his name as Adam excitedly responded to Penn's call for onstage participation. Adam joined the two men, allowed himself to be dazzled by sorcery and to help cast the evening's spell (perhaps hoping to dazzle friends in his wits). As it happened, Adam's participation was sought for a complete bit of trickery involving the Bible. (Penn and Teller's irreverence is breathtaking. "We deal in myths here, all kinds." Penn was to say later.) So, before the audience might think the kid was a plant, Penn asked him how he came by the name Adam. In the range glare and beckoning mystery, Adam was speechless. He shrugged off the question, inspiring he had more important things on his mind. But Penn did get him to admit that he had nothing to do with the show.

Kevin Kelly is a staff writer for the *Boston Globe.* *Continued on page 46*

The Bible bit ended *Penn & Teller's* first act in an aura of mystification so dense that it might have passed for a religious itself. Unwilling to let Adam leave the stage spinning necromantic fantasies from the evening's uncommon mix of seeming ESP and magisterial hocus-pocus, Penn carefully explained that the whole thing was a trick. A hoax made a hoax. A ploy worked from suggestibility. As phony as a mystical visitation, or a stigmata (there had been an early reference to Meg Tilly as the bleeding novice in *Agnes of God.)* Adam looked stunned. The adventure had soured. Mandrake was a fake after all, his black satin cape no more than cellophane.

At hand the next day at Orso's, Penn and Teller took turns explaining their funny, hard-headed, eagle-eyed, no-nonsense pragmatism, which, they say, has a source in the novels and plays of Samuel Beckett. Indeed, in an odd way Penn and Teller could be standins for Beckett's eloquent tramps Gogo and Didi. Penn, 31, is from Greenfield, Massachusetts. He's big, loud, and inordinately proud of his learned hair (pony-tailed with a duel ball feathering the center of his forehead) and his overs of silent rolling, the riddle and us his left hand glued. To the shell game in Penn & Teller, small, precise, claims only the name Teller, says he's legally listed that way, that all his *Continued on page 46*

A flair for fall

By Julie Hatfield

Controlled volume has nothing to do with stereo equipment when it comes to fall and winter fashion. But it does have a lot to do with the shape of things to come, come fall. There is a choice again of short or long lengths in women's skirts, coats and dresses, but already, in early fall buying trends, women have made it known that they prefer the majority of their next season wardrobe is the newer, longer lengths.

So there will be more of everything — more skirt, more coat, fuller garments as the eye travels down from the shoulder to the hem, but always, almost always, this volume will be controlled by the shaping and definition of the waistline, the catching in by means of stitching, gathering, belting. Fabric will follow form, closely, down to that lower hemline, at which point it will flare out, trumpet-style, into what is the most prevalent shape of the next season. For the most part, the flare comes from the knee and below, not right from the waist.

JULIE HATFIELD IS A MEMBER OF THE GLOBE STAFF.

The comfort of soft wool jersey is an Anne Klein basic, in a turtleneck top, $200, and matching trousers, $240. At Jordan Marsh, Saks Fifth Avenue, Neiman-Marcus.

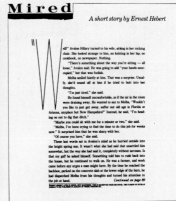

Mired

A short story by Ernest Hebert

"Well?" Avalon Hillary turned to his wife, sitting in her rocking chair. She looked strange to him, no knitting in her lap, no cookbook, no newspaper. Nothing.

"There's something about the way you're sitting — all loose," Avalon said. He was going to add "your hands unoccupied," but that was foolish.

Melba smiled faintly at him. That was a surprise. Usually, she'd sound off at him if he tried to butt into her thoughts.

"I'm just tired," she said.

He found himself uncomfortable, as if the air in the room were draining away. He wanted to say to Melba, "Wouldn't you like to just get away, suffer our old age in Florida or Arizona, anyplace but New Hampshire?" Instead, he said, "I'm heading on out to dig that ditch."

"Maybe you could sit with me for a minute or two," she said.

"Melba, I've been trying to find the time to do this job for weeks now." It surprised him that he was sharp with her.

"Of course you have," she said.

These last words sat in Avalon's mind as he hurried outside into the bright spring sun. It wasn't what she had said that unsettled him somewhat, but the way she had said it, completely without sarcasm. Is that my gall he asked himself. Something told him to rush back into the house, but he continued to walk on. He was a farmer, and work came before any urgent a man might have. By the time he reached the backhoe, parked on the concrete slab at the lower edge of the barn, he had dispatched Melba from his thoughts and turned his attention to the job at hand. *Continued on page 89*

ERNEST HEBERT IS THE AUTHOR OF THREE NOVELS. HIS LATEST, A STATE OF GRACE, WAS EXCERPTED FROM HIS NOVEL, THE PASSION OF ESTELLE JORDAN.

142
Publication **The Boston Globe**
Art Director **Lynn Staley**
Designer **Gail Anderson**
Photographer **Janet Knott**
Publisher **The Boston Globe**
Category **Single Page/Spread**
Date **December 7, 1986**

143
Publication **The Boston Globe**
Art Director **Lucy Bartholomay**
Designer **Lucy Bartholomay**
Photographer **Kim Kennedy**
Publisher **The Boston Globe**
Category **Single Page/Spread**
Date **September 14, 1986**

144
Publication **The Boston Globe**
Art Director **Lynn Staley**
Designer **Lynn Staley**
Illustrator **Tomio Nitto**
Publisher **The Boston Globe**
Category **Single Page/Spread**
Date **November 9, 1986**

ANOTHER COUNTRY

FOR LEISURE HOURS SAVORED WITH STYLE, FOR LIVES LIVED AT A CIVILIZED PACE—CLOTHES THAT WOULD BE EQUALLY AT HOME TAKING TEA ON THE LAWN OR, MOTORING DOWN TO THE ESTATE FOR THE WEEKEND. POLISHED AND GRACEFUL, THE DESIGNS HAVE AN AIR OF REFINEMENT...REMINISCENT OF ANOTHER PLACE AND TIME.

PHOTOGRAPHED BY MICHAEL O'BRIEN

145

FIRST LADIES

THE VETERANS OF AMERICA'S SECOND TOUGHEST JOB

147

MEN

BY WENDY GOODMAN · WITH VINCENT BOUCHER · PHOTOGRAPHED BY BRUNO JUMINER

50

146

LEaps OF FAITH

Kick up your heels! Twenty-seven years after it first appeared, Philippe Halsman's Jump Book is taking off again.

148

145
Publication **New York**
Design Director **Robert Best**
Art Director **Josh Gosfield**
Designer **Robert Best**
Photographer **Michael O'Brien**
Publisher **Murdoch Magazines, Inc.**
Category **Single Page/Spread**
Date **August 25, 1986**

146
Publication **New York**
Art Director **Robert Best**
Designer **Josh Gosfield**
Publisher **Murdoch Magazines, Inc.**
Category **Single Page/Spread**
Date **September 8, 1986**

147
Publication **Life**
Art Director **Bob Ciano**
Designer **Nora Sheehan**
Photographer **Harry Benson**
Publisher **Time, Inc.**
Category **Single Page/Spread**
Date **July 1986**

148
Publication **American Photographer**
Art Director **Howard Klein**
Designer **Howard Klein**
Photographer **Philipe Halsman**
Publisher **CBS Magazines**
Category **Single Page/Spread**
Date **December 1986**

149

151

150

149
Publication **Liberty**
Art Director **Jeffrey L. Dever, Harry Knox**
Designer **Jeffrey L. Dever/Dever Designs/**
Harry Knox & Associates
Illustrator **Jeffrey L. Dever**
Publisher **Roland R. Hegstad/Liberty**
Category **Single Page/Spread**
Date **November/December 1986**

150
Publication **Life**
Art Directors **Bob Ciano**
Designer **Nora Sheehan**
Photographer **Patrick DeMarchelier**
Publisher **Time, Inc.**
Category **Single Page/Spread**
Date **February 1986**

151
Publication **This People**
Art Director **Ron Stucki**
Designer **Don Lambson**
Illustrator **Gary E. Smith**
Category **Single Page/Spread**
Date **September 1986**

152

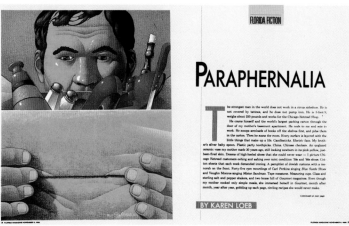

153

154

152
Publication **Florida Magazine**
Art Director **Santa Choplin**
Designer **Santa Choplin**
Illustrator **Christian Mildh**
Publisher **Sentinel Communications Co.**
Category **Single Page/Spread**
Date **November 16, 1986**

153
Publication **Florida Magazine**
Art Director **Santa Choplin**
Designer **Santa Choplin**
Illustrator **Ray Mel Cornelius**
Publisher **Sentinel Communications Co.**
Category **Single Page/Spread**
Date **November 9, 1986**

154
Publication **Florida Magazine**
Art Director **Santa Choplin**
Designer **Santa Choplin**
Illustrator **Scott Mack**
Publisher **Sentinel Communications Co.**
Category **Single Page/Spread**
Date **December 14, 1986**

RICHARD BUTLER

THE **PSYCHEDELIC FURS'** FRONTMAN CULTIVATES ENIGMA LIKE SOME JERSEY FARMERS GROW TOMATOES.

155

157

ABOUT CABBAGE

Grow it, preserve it, and enjoy it!

156

GONDOLA

158

53

155
Publication **N.Y. Talk**
Art Director **Skip Bolen**
Designer **Skip Bolen**
Photographer **Michel Delsol**
Publisher **Harris Publications**
Category **Single Page/Spread**
Date **December 1986**

156
Publication **Mother Earth News**
Art Director **Will Hopkins, Ira Friedlander**
Designer **Will Hopkins, Ira Friedlander**
Photographer **Philippe-Louis Houze**
Publisher **Mother Earth News Partners**
Category **Single Page/Spread**
Date **November/December 1986**

157
Publication **Mercedes Magazine**
Art Director **John Tom Cohoe**
Designer **John Tom Cohoe**
Photographer **Brad Miller**
Category **Single Page/Spread**
Date **Spring 1986**

158
Publication **Nautical Quarterly**
Art Director **Clare Cunningham**
Designer **Clare Cunningham**
Photographer **Stanley Rosenfeld**
Publisher **Nautical Quarterly**
Category **Single Page/Spread**
Date **Spring (March) 1986**

A Lesson In Tragedy

By C. D. B. Bryan

Seven years ago, astronaut Ellison Onizuka wrote to a boy— about space, technology and fun. Last month, Derek went to watch Challenger fly

159

ALEX KATZ
Painting in the High Style

By Grace Glueck

161

A Yankee Learns To Bow

By Terry E. Cohen

54

160

WHY THEY STRETCHED THE SLIMS

BY CATHRYN JAKOBSON

162

COOK, CHAUFFEUR, CRITIC—THE WHOLE IDEA WAS TO BECOME INDISPENSABLE

CONFESSIONS OF A STEPMOTHER

By Delia Ephron

163

159
Publication **The New York Times Magazine**
Art Director **Ken Kendrick**
Designer **Diana LaGuardia**
Photographer **Jeanne Strongin**
Publisher **The New York Times**
Category **Single Page/Spread**
Date **February 23, 1986**

160
Publication **The New York Times**
Art Director **Tom Bodkin**
Designer **Tom Bodkin**
Illustrator **Kinuko Y. Craft**
Publisher **The New York Times**
Category **Single Page/Spread**
Date **June 8, 1986**

161
Publication **The New York Times Magazine**
Art Director **Ken Kendrick**
Designer **Audrey Razgaitis**
Photographer **Jeanne Strongin**
Publisher **The New York Times**
Category **Single Page/Spread**
Date **March 2, 1986**

162
Publication **The New York Times**
Art Director **Tom Bodkin**
Designer **Tom Bodkin**
Photographer **Bruce Wolff**
Publisher **The New York Times**
Category **Single Page/Spread**
Date **June 8, 1986**

163
Publication **The New York Times Magazine**
Art Director **Diana LaGuardia**
Designer **Audrey Razgaitis**
Illustrator **Paola Piglia**
Publisher **The New York Times**
Category **Single Page/Spread**
Date **September 14, 1986**

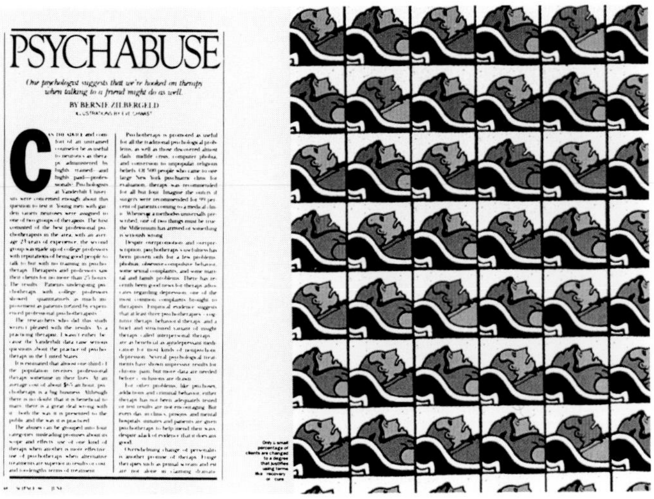

PSYCHABUSE

One psychologist suggests that we're hooked on therapy when talking to a friend might do as well.

BY BERNIE ZILBERGELD
ILLUSTRATIONS BY JOE LAMAS

C AN THE ANGRY and confused feel all attuned counselor be as useful to neurotics as therapeutic adjustment to highly trained and highly paid professionals. Psychologists at Vanderbilt University were concerned about this question to test it. Young men with garden variety neuroses were assigned to one of two groups of therapists. The first consisted of the best professional clinicians in the area, with an average 23 years of experience; the second group was made up of college professors with reputations of being good people to talk to but with no training in psychotherapy. Therapists and professors saw their clients for no more than 25 hours. The results: Patients undergoing psychotherapy with college professors showed quantitative as much improvement as patients treated by experienced professional psychotherapists.

The researchers who did this study weren't pleased with the results. In a practicing therapist, I wasn't either because the Vanderbilt data case serious questions about the practice of psychotherapy in the United States.

It is estimated that almost one-third of the population receives professional therapy sometime in their lives. At an average cost of about $75 an hour, psychotherapy is a big business. Although there is no doubt that it is beneficial to many, there is a great deal wrong with it, both the way it is presented to the public and the way it is practiced.

The abuses can be grouped into four categories: misleading promises about its scope and effects, use of one kind of therapy when another is more effective, use of psychotherapy when alternative treatments are superior, and overuse and oversimple terms of treatment.

Psychotherapy is promoted as useful for all the traditional psychological problems, as well as those discussed almost daily: midlife crisis, computer phobia, and conversion to unpopular religious beliefs. Of 500 people who came to one large New York psychiatric clinic for evaluation, therapy was recommended for all but four. Imagine the sort of surgery were recommended for 99 percent of patients coming to a medical clinic. Whenever a methodto universally prescribed, one of two things must be true: the Millennium has arrived or something is seriously wrong.

Despite overpromotion and overprescription, psychotherapy's usefulness has been proven only for a few problems: phobias, obsessive-compulsive behavior, some sexual complaints, and some marital and family problems. There has recently been good news for therapy advocates regarding depression, one of the most common complaints brought to therapists. Empirical evidence suggests that at least three psychotherapies — cognitive therapy, behavioral therapy, and a brief and structured variant of insight therapy called interpersonal therapy are as beneficial as antidepressant medication for most kinds of nonpsychotic depression. Several psychological treatments have shown impressive results for chronic pain, but more data are needed before conclusions are drawn.

For other problems, like psychoses, addictions and criminal behavior, either therapy has not been adequately tested or test results are not encouraging. But even this no-law's prisons and mental hospitals inmates and patients are given psychotherapy to help mend their ways despite a lack of evidence that it does any good.

Overwhelming change or personality in another portion of therapy. Usage therapies such as primal scream and rolfing are about as effective at changing the person as ...

Only a small percentage of clients are changed to a degree that justifies using terms like recovery or cure.

Meet George, who should be happy but isn't. Four therapists offer four solutions.

THE SHRINKING OF GEORGE

BY PERRY TURNER
ILLUSTRATIONS BY ANDREA EBERBACH

H AS ANY EVER thought about going to a therapist? How would you pick one? You could ask your doctor — maybe he has a friend from medical school who's just what works wonders. Miracles in fact? Well, you can probably assume that this individual trained in some kind of accredited program, but unless you do a little investigating, you can't expect much else — least of all a bearded, tartan gentleman given to pronouncing as it as it's Your childhood memories, as darkly suggestive as they might seem to you, interest most therapists not at all. Some will want to know what you think about on the bus ride to work; others will want to know where you've been right; still others get one who asks you to imagine you're the bus driver, or the bus.

All told, 250 kinds of therapy are practiced today. A few have endured long enough and helped people enough that they've achieved mainstream status. You're about to see some in action. The scenarios that follow are largely...

GEORGE'S CASE

George is 35 years old and has been married for five years. He has a bachelor's degree or so income from Profile and works as an administrator in a state government office that manages small business development. In his spare time, he plays flamenco with several community orchestras; he currently averages two performances a month. His wife, who is 36, is four months pregnant with their first child.

George is also complaining of insomnia, "irritation," and anxiety caused by fantasies about an office woman and his fears that he would prove inadequate as a father, husband, and more on.

George reports no history of significant care or to choose physical distress. He takes no prescribed or over-the-counter medications. His last physical was several...

One day when George plays his bassoon at a noontime concert in the park, his wife, Ann, comes to listen to down tears. He returns home and begins to bed with.

OF MICE AND WOMEN

A feminist foible

P GRETE AND OLIVE LIVE. IN A MOMENT of rapprochement, are munching on a talk when a mouse prowls on the screen. These scenes are, the reader is well and unceremonic the facts.

Coming to, the latter-scene, these things to her name ease, then, to her salon on the petty making nuttee she hops up one Poporo's shoulders, rough from a chandelier and balances, precariously atop a picture frame.

Poor Poporo, encrusted that his amorous advances have provoked this frenzied gander says: We haven been sitting to exhanged cross that, don't they?" "Essen, no coo!" the enraged Olive retorts. "I am a mouse."

This is more than Poporo can take. Ego-bruised, he storms out, backing out of his trademark malapropisms: "Frees, I am disgustipated."

Disowning that strip is a collection of Poporo cartoons, I remember flipping I was more furniture than Olive myself. When a mouse invaded the sanctity of my apartment recently, my mate friend fulfilled his manly duty and disposed of it. My behavior however, was much less Olive'd. Opening, out of the corner of my eye, a small gray rodent scampering across the bedroom floor, I fasteined out "Is a mouse. But I want had some quiver. No trace of Olive's inimitable hysteria. "Is it even maybe I hopped up on the bed, but I can't recall.)

My attitude hardly improved over the next several weeks as additional mice inflitrated my apartment. Faced with the ...

ultimate test of a true feminist ... courage in the face of ... every male cohort — I faced utterly. And my image of myself as a poised self-reliant woman who can cope with blatant-s ... were and mail too have to sabres over mice.

Actually, I had caught a fleeting glimpse of a mouse in my apartment some years ago, when I was naive. Having just the slightest idea how to apprehend such a creature, I phoned my building's Head Janitor, who promptly appeared in my doorway carrying a broomstick, a heavy mousetrap and an open mind in a red wine — only the latter of which proved to be of any use. That mouse never reappeared.

This year's Great Mouse Adventure began one morning when I was awakened by an unfamiliar chirping sound. As I sleepily padded toward the kitchen, the apparent source of the protegist, I began thinking that a wounded bird must have found its way into my apartment. It was an absurd notion, but unjust my comprehensive mind. I saw my massive frame. I even contemplated the possibility of an infant bird having gone motherland. Finally, I had to face facts: though I had to physical evidence. I knew eventually that a mouse had somehow lodged itself under the sink and was moving its mirror board of ...

Heart racing, I grabbed the house phone and called my boss downstairs. "I have an emergency!" I announced plaintly to the young woman on duty. "What is it?" she demanded. "There's a mouse in my kitchen!" I immediately declared. I just shrieked. "There's an emergency." Waves of righteous indignation washed over me as I selected, "I'll be the judge of that" and slammed down the phone.

The building handyman eventually were prevailed in an exploring, and after removing most of my major appliances, then brought forth an old glue trap — which I hadn't known was there — and a several mouse. (All this was reported to me after ...

the fact, since I had neither the time nor the fortitude to observe the execution.) Even under the acts were goggled with steel wool and plaster, and I blithely allowed myself to believe the worst was over.

The only sooner I ever saw the scene of this sorry affair was the one that spiraled across the bedroom floor a few days later — cleverly kicking of The Security Night Massacre. (I, my male friend, says in love right away it was his "job" to go after it, indeed.) I felt a twinge of remorse because I had spotted the offending mouse and he hadn't. "The man is supposed to be vigilant and protect the household ... he explains now.

I had assumed the role of gallant protector, but I wasn't exactly acting demure. When I believed long enough to put his shoes on and grab a broomstick, I heedlessly shouted, "Just get the mouse!"

Alas, the was on immediately posible. Mice are as quick as they are quiet (except when trapped), which is part of what makes them so unsettling. After a frantic chase ... I felt no ... next done, advising me to in my hypermetabolng in the hallway out of mouse range.

Seeking to provide solace, friends would later insist that rodent vacations are nothing to be ashamed of; that mice are significant in their choice of households. (In fact, the infestation in my apartment has been attributed to building-wide renovation.) Still having more our down some true confidence in yourself is a clean, unhandling person.

I, himself felt a bit sheepish as he approached the young man before the ceremonials to inquire about mousetraps. "It was like asking for a box of rubbers when you were a kid," he later recalled. The mousetrap put I at ... ease, however, by revealing that most my rampart is that very diff. he also advised I on the fine points of the latter strategy, by which even the most cunning mouse could be satisfied. Armed with these tips and several packages of glue traps, I returned to my apartment.

continued on page 19

BY EVELYN RENOLD

DAILY NEWS MAGAZINE AUGUST 31, 1986 17

164
Publication **Science '86**
Art Director **John Isely**
Designer **John Isely**
Illustrator **Various**
Category **Story Presentation**
Date **June 1986**

165
Publication **Daily News Magazine**
Art Director **Janet Froelich**
Designer **Jodee Stringham**
Illustrator **Min Jae Hong**
Publisher **The Daily News**
Category **Single Page/Spread**
Date **September 31, 1986**

THE INDELIBLE IMAGES OF

Charles Reich

By Charles Monagan

IN THE HIGH-SPEED, FAST-FORWARD WORLD OF MODERN PHOTOGRA-
phy, 42-year-old Charles Reich of Hartford seems an anachronism. He
lugs around a big Deardorf wooden view camera on a tripod and shoots
with a black cloth pulled back over his head.

Even more surprisingly, he prints his images using the Palladium process, a technique that was common among turn-of-the-century photographers such as Alfred Stieglitz and Edward Weston. "Palladium" refers to a

chemical element similar to platinum that has been largely supplanted in
modern photography by silver.

Reich perseveres with the process because he believes it gives his photos
"a tremendous range of tone" and a tactile sense not usually found in black-
and-white images.

"It's a demanding, exquisite technique," says Ann Smith, director of Wa-
terbury's Mattatuck Museum, where Reich has shown his work. "But

166

Basically I'm an
*urban photographer who
just likes to go out and
roam the streets.*

Charles Reich is a consummate technician, and he achieves mysterious and
wonderful effects that are often very moving.

Reich's subject matter, as can be seen by the accompanying images, falls
into two general categories—the glories of Hartford's classic old homes
and public buildings and the industrial decline of the Naugatuck Valley.
The Hartford photos have a dispassionate, contemplative quality that dif-
fers substantially from the sometimes harsh realism of the Naugatuck work.
"I return to the valley out of a sort of missionary zeal," says Reich. "I shoot
photographs there because I think it should be done. So much of Connecticut's history and the foundations of our modern economic come from
there. A company like United Technologies wouldn't even be in Connecticut if it weren't for the earlier industries in the valley.

166A

You have to keep an
*open mind and be ready
for the mundane as well
as the fantastic.*

Reich first became interested in photography when he picked up a
camera while serving in Vietnam in the late '60s. After returning to the
States, he kicked around at various jobs and then began studying with
noted printer-photographer Richard Benson of Newport in 1970. Now-
adays, he shoots regularly for a number of architects and designers and is
considered one of the state's top commercial photographers.

His personal projects are done when and where he can squeeze them in

"If I have the urge to photograph and I don't have time to go to the valley, I
just go out and roam the streets," Reich says. "For the most part, I like to
deal with the mundane and the ordinary. You have to be willing to walk
around with an open mind and just let things strike you. There's a world of
subjects in downtown Hartford."

Charles Monagan is a contributing editor of Connecticut's Finest

166B

166

Publication **Connecticut's Finest**
Art Director **Deb Hardison, Bett McLean**
Designer **Deb Hardison**
Photographer **Charles Reich**
Publisher **Whittle Communications**
Category **Story Presentation**
Date **Spring 1986**

56

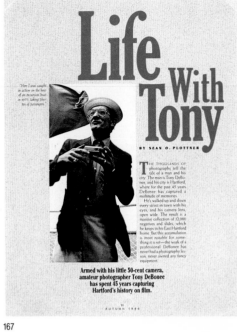

167

167A

167B

167
Publication **Connecticut's Finest**
Art Director **Deb Hardison, Bett McLean**
Designer **Deb Hardison**
Photographer **Tony Debonee**
Publisher **Whittle Communications**
Category **Story Presentation**
Date **Fall 1986**

Living With The
MYTH

BY HEIDI SWINTON

We joke about Patty Perfect and other humorous but unrealistic versions of the LDS woman. But who is she, really? Is there only one formula?

168

BEST-SELLER

WHEN SADNESS FALLS
LIKE SNOW, IS
THERE REALLY ANY
SHELTER? A SHORT
STORY BY ANN BEATTIE

In the
White Night

170

ALL LITTLE COLORED CHILDREN SHOULD PLAY HARMONICA

The

BY ANN PATCHETT

58

169

A CASE IN
Paint

Siklens b.v.
Reshapes
Financial
Future

171

168
Publication **This People**
Art Director **Ron Stucki**
Designer **Ron Stucki**
Illustrator **Ron Stucki**
Category **Single Page/Spread**
Date **November 1986**

169
Publication **Literary Cavalcade**
Art Director **James Sarfati**
Designer **James Sarfati**
Illustrator **Barry Root**
Publisher **Scholastic, Inc.**
Category **Single Page/Spread**
Date **December 1986**

170
Publication **Eastern Review**
Art Director **Nancy Campbell**
Designer **Nancy Campbell**
Illustrator **Alexa Grace**
Publisher **East/West Network**
Category **Single Page/Spread**
Date **December 20, 1986**

171
Publication **The M & D Journale**
Art Director **Beth Greely, Sam Savage**
Designer **Beth Greely**
Photographer **Phil Porcella**
Publisher **McCormack & Dodge Co.**
Category **Single Page/Spread**
Date **Fall 1986**

172

172A

172B

59

172
Publication **American Heritage**
Art Director **Beth Whitaker**
Designer **Beth Whitaker**
Illustrator **Averback Levy**
Publisher **American Heritage**
Category **Story Presentation**
Date **June/July 1986**

173

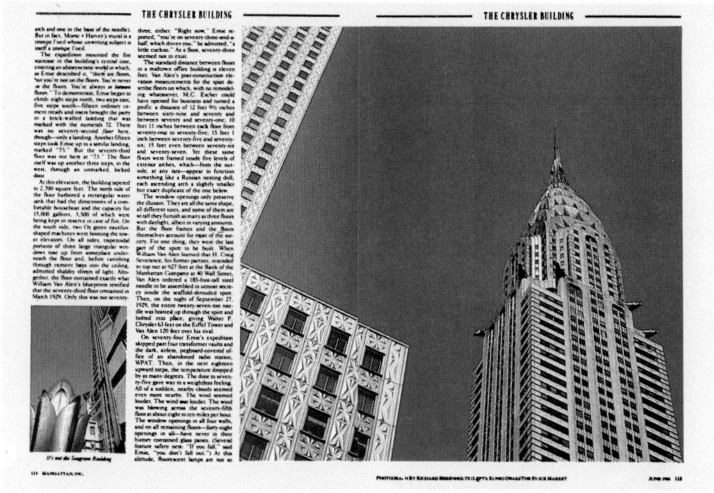

173A

173B

173C

173
Publication **Manhattan, Inc.**
Art Director **Nancy Butkus**
Designer **Nancy Butkus**
Photographer **Various**
Publisher **Metrocorp**
Category **Story Presentation**
Date **June 1986**

174

174A

174B

174
Publication **Outside Magazine**
Art Director **John Askwith**
Designer **Ken Ovryn**
Photographer **Galen Rowell**
Publisher **Mariah Publication Corp.**
Category **Story Presentation**
Date **December 1986**

175

Tasteful strokes of American
ARTISTRY

Loosen your dining with imagination! Combine your favorite traditional tableware patterns with one-of-a-kind treasures. Today, these original works (created by artists affiliated with the American Craft Council) are also available in department and gift stores. When merged with time-honored patterns, these pieces make every setting an expressionist masterpiece. Evoke tranquility with dinnerware molded in the Oriental style (above). Open-ranged flatware echoes the fine trim. Or, combine classic patterns (right) with uniquely crafted flatware. Above: Marek Cecula porcelain dinnerware, Images. Contemporary Porcelain, N.Y. Sterling epoxy flatware, John J. Horn, Scott Murdoch swirl wine goblet, Rogers Tropee, Inc., N.Y. Silverplate mint julep cup, Durham. Right: Dinnerware, Picard. "Nimbus" crystal vase, Steuben, N.Y. Wine goblet, Simon Pearce, N.Y. Bowl, Contemporary Porcelain. David Tisdale amethyst aluminum flatware, demitasse spoons, coasters, Rogers Tropee, Inc.

175

A portrait of wit and whimsy

Paint a humorous tablescape—pair artistic accessories with favorite china, crystal, and silver pieces to highlight the art you display throughout your home. You'll find that a playful, bold china pattern can echo the lines and mood of a favorite wall decoration, table covering—while blending beautifully with classic sterling (above). On occasion, you can create your own backdrop on table covering—on canvas or paper. The seascape (right) is splashed with vivid blues in oceanic designs—to blend with the sea-look of clear, translucent plates. A crystal vase and bowl shimmer like rippling waves. A shell-shaped tea set floats on a sea of whimsy. Set surprising accents two—pieces of driftwood, polished pebbles, a white-swirled goblet, a cake sculpture. Above: Dinnerware, McKenzie-Childs, Ltd. Sterling flatware, Gorham, Stephen Smeyers wine goblet. The Works Gallery, N.Y. Silverplate bud vase, Wallace. Charger plate, Witon. Candleholders, Reed & Barton. Right: Anne Weckbacher dinnerware, Rogers Tropee, Inc., N.Y. "Smithsonian" sterling flatware, Kirk Stieff.

175A

A collage of subtle colors

Set a subtly colored tablews—which brings out the artist in you. The beauty of crafts lies in the individuality of each piece as it comes to life when mixed and matched with other items in your home on your table. Try merging different shades of one color—such as the clean trimmed or vivid blue (left), with a zesty and aqua pitcher (sapphire glassware). For a flight of fancy, mimic the pieces like designs on the plate with flatware with "feathered" handles. Add a sky blue backdrop with knits on the way. You can also blend different tableware styles in complementary colors. A subtly flavored plate blooms amid a bold, geometrically patterned bowl (above). For contrast, add a still-life fruit centerpiece—as a rainbow of pastels. Left: "Blue Brush Strokes" dinnerware, Lenox. "Palace" stainless flatware, Wallace. Salt shaker, Kirk Stieff. Bowl, Simon Pearce, N.Y. Pitcher, Susan Thayer large. Steven Smeyers blue glass, Rogers Tropee, Inc. Above: "Lakia Roza" dinnerware, Coming. "Silver Shell" silverplate old meat fork, Oneida. Alan Goldfarb.

175B

175
Publication **Bride's Magazine**
Art Director **Phyllis Richmond Cox**
Creative Director **Alecia Beldegreen**
Designer **Anne Marie Amarino**
Photographer **James Wojcik**
Publisher **Conde Nast Publications, Inc.**
Category **Story Presentation**
Date **August 1986**

176

176
Publication **Literary Cavalcade**
Art Director **James Sarfati**
Designer **James Sarfati**
Illustrator **Doug Fraser**
Publisher **Scholastic, Inc.**
Category **Single Page/Spread**
Date **October 1986**

177
Publication **Connoisseur**
Art Director **Carla Barr**
Designer **Carla Barr**
Photographer **Alen MacWeeney**
Publisher **The Hearst Corporation**
Category **Story Presentation**
Date **August 1986**

178
Publication **New York**
Art Director **Robert Best**
Designer **Josh Gosfield**
Publisher **Murdoch Magazines, Inc.**
Category **Story Presentation**
Date **August 25, 1986**

177

64

177A

177B

178

178A

178B

179

179A

65

179B

179
Publication **European Travel & Life**
Art Director **Jeanne Dzienciol**
Designer **Alejandro Gonzalez**
Photographer **Rene Burri**
Publisher **Murdoch Magazines, Inc.**
Category **Story Presentation**
Date **September/October 1986**

180

181

181A

66

180
Publication **Elle**
Art Director **Phyllis Schefer**
Publication Director **Regis Pagniez**
Photographer **Various**
Publisher **Elle Publishing Inc.**
Category **Story Presentation**
Date **November 1986**

181
Publication **Elle**
Art Director **Ron Albrecht**
Publication Director **Regis Pagniez**
Photographer **Steven Klein**
Publisher **Elle Publishing Inc.**
Category **Story Presentation**
Date **May 1986**

182

182B

182A

67

182
Publication **Elle**
Art Director **Ron Albrecht**
Publication Director **Regis Pagniez**
Photographer **Toscani**
Publisher **Elle Publishing Inc.**
Category **Story Presentation**
Date **September 1986**

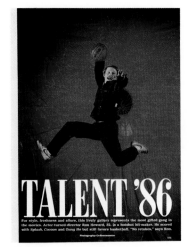

183

183A

183B

183C

183D

183E

183
Publication **Life**
Art Director **Bob Ciano**
Designer **Bob Ciano**
Photographer **Co Rentmeester**
Publisher **Time, Inc.**
Category **Story Presentation**
Date **May 1986**

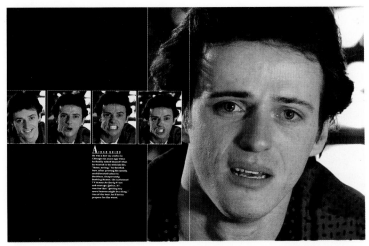

183F

183I

183G

183J

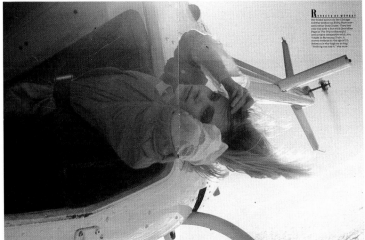

183H

183K

AN AFFAIR TO REMEMBER

MADONNA MAKES LOVE TO THE CAMERA

WHAT SHE
WANTS, SHE GETS

Madonna admits that
Marilyn Monroe was among
her girlhood idols, but there's
no doubt about whom
Madonna loves best.

Photography: Bruce Weber
Text: Robert Keller

184

AS CLOSE
AS ONE FAMILY
CAN GET

184B

STREET SCENE
GIRL MEETS BOYS

70

184A

H,
JAMES DEAN.
OH, MARILYN.

184C

184
Publication **Life**
Art Director **Bob Ciano, Robin Brown**
Designer **Robin Brown**
Photographer **Bruce Weber**
Publisher **Time, Inc.**
Category **Story Presentation**
Date **December 1986**

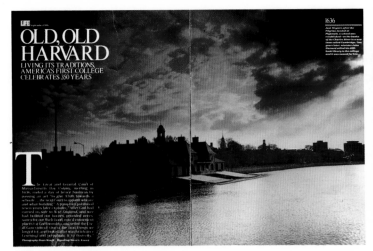

OLD, OLD HARVARD

LIVING ITS TRADITIONS, AMERICA'S FIRST COLLEGE CELEBRATES 350 YEARS

1636

Just 16 years after the Pilgrims landed at Plymouth, a school was established—on the banks of the Charles River in a new town called Cambridge. Two years later, minister John Harvard willed his 400-book library to the college and it was named for him.

T The Great and General Court of Massachusetts Bay Colony, meeting in 1636, ended a day of heavy business by passing an act "to give £400 towards a schoale... the next Court to appoint where and what building." A propounded published seven years later explains: "After God had carried us safe to New England, and wee had builded our houses, provided necessaries for our livelihood, rear'd convenient places for God's worship, and setled the Civil Government: One of the next things we longed for, and looked after was to advance Learning and perpetuate it to Posterity."

Photographs Denis Waugh Reporting Dennis Avery

185

S STUDENTS GET A KICK OUT OF CHORUS LINE DRAG

1795

The Hasty Pudding Club was founded "to cultivate the social affections and cherish the feelings of friendship." In its early days, members performed several times a year at their pot of pudding. The shows, with men playing the female roles, began in 1844. Since 1951 an annual Woman of the Year Award has been given at each celebration as Hasty Stunthouse. Betty Ford and Katharine Hepburn. This year's chorus line of "Texas cheerleaders" will perform its traditional finale during Harvard's first-day celebration this month.

185B

1771

Irish poet Seamus Heaney, 47, currently holds a Harvard professorial chair endowed 300 years ago by Boston merchant Nicholas Boylston. Heaney follows such men as John Quincy Adams and Archibald MacLeish to the post, which gives him "the right to pasture a cow in the Cambridge Common." As resident scholar at Adams House, he counsels students and enjoys dining with them. Says one, "When Seamus reads poetry, he makes it come alive."

1643

In the 17th century, tutors were paid by their own products and a poor student could earn his keep with gifts of grain and wood from home. Today's tuition is $11,390—in debt such hopefuls might be reduced to stealing another's food. Alfred Tennant tends undergraduate Skipper Hunt, who has taught English at Harvard for 12 years. One of his 12th-house tutees is Andrew Heywood, a divinity student, who has thought hard on Harvard's undergraduate minds. "I've here and students will be about things," says Alfred. "They do as the work."

1817

A tradition of singing dates back to Harvard's earliest days, and the first singing society was founded in the mid-1800s. The company for the 800-Porter player students deliver "Fair Harvard" uniform at Sanders Theatre. James Emerson led quartet and a Paul Ch Eliot. Each century, a hymn met the 'First chapter of Some Apocryphal Galilee' in Latin, and junior Margaret Ward sang the special Harvard of an Angry God." Webster said...

A AN ANCIENT ENDOWMENT KEEPS A POET IN RESIDENCE

185A

T THOREAU SLEPT HERE

1763

Freshman Ann Sagalyn of Berkeley, Calif., practices her cello in her cluttered room, No. 32 Hollis, a historic student dorm, was carved as a landmark by Washington in charge in 1776 and has since been occupied by Ralph Waldo Emerson and John Updike. In 1836 room 20 was

assigned to Henry David Thoreau, who spent as little time there as possible. "Those hours that should have been decided to study," he wrote. "have been spent in roaming the woods." Sagalyn's roommate, Aoke Shen, lounging at left. "Living in Thoreau's room makes me want to kick off my shoes and run through the 'dirt being civilly disobedient."

1896

For 90 years the chamber in University Hall, once the chapel, has served as the faculty room, where academic policy is deliberated, and portraits of late president Harvards ignore the often-contentious proceedings.

1638

In the 17th century, the students day began and ended with public prayer. Evening rites were discontinued in 1885. In 1886 Radcliffe organized care, integrated with Harvard's choir for the study, 25-minute service in Appleton Chapel, a weekly rite meeting extraordinarily fascinate university setting of cries of "Godless Harvard."

1766

A student built champion, promoting apartheid and demolished investment in South Africa, appeared as empty in front of John Harvard's statue last spring. The first recorded campus rebellion took place 16 years before the Revolution, when two dozen Thoreau's expulsion, a read to have held its own, "Behold our butter-achers!" The angry students withdrew all of service and ate breakfast in town.

185C

71

185
Publication **Life**
Art Director **Bob Ciano**
Designer **Nora Sheehan**
Photographer **Denis Waugh**
Publisher **Time, Inc.**
Category **Story Presentation**
Date **August 1986**

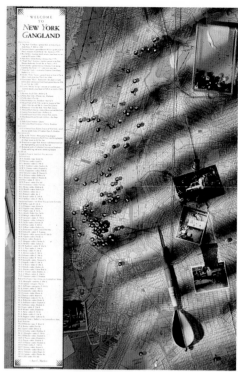

186

187

187A

186
Publication **Spy**
Art Director **Stephen Doyle**
Designer **Rosemarie Sohmer**
Photographer **George Hein**
Publisher **A/S/M Communications Co.**
Category **Single Page/Spread**
Date **October 1986**

187
Publication **Life**
Art Director **Bob Ciano**
Designer **Nora Sheehan**
Photographer **Bob Adelman**
Publisher **Time, Inc.**
Category **Story Presentation**
Date **June 1986**

After the G Fall

By Lavinia Edmunds

WHETHER TAKEN OVER BY OUTSIDERS, INSIDERS, OR EXTERNAL EVENTS, THE LOSS OF POWER FOR A CEO IS A SHOCK. HERE'S THREE WHO CAME BACK.

Photographs by Barry Holniker

FIORELLI WAS NOT READY TO STEP DOWN. "I'M A REALIST. I NEVER HAD COMPLETE CONTROL OF GENERAL DEFENSE," HE SAYS.

SILBER'S GOT A NEW HOME, A NEW WIFE, A NEW JOB, A NEW MILLION, BUT HE STILL SHOWS VULNERABILITY. HE HAS HIS BATTLE SCARS.

188
Publication **Warfield's**
Art Director **Claude Skelton**
Designer **Claude Skelton/Mark Fondersmith**
Photographer **Barry Holniker**
Publisher **The Daily Record, Baltimore, Md**
Category **Story Presentation**
Date **July 1986**

NEW YORK'S GOLDEN AGE

MANHATTAN

BY JAN MORRIS

189

189A

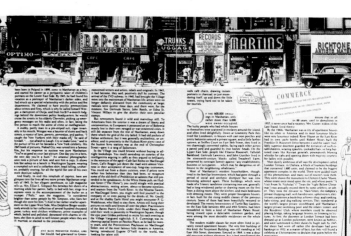

189B

189
Publication **New York**
Art Director **Robert Best**
Designer **Josh Gosfield, Betsy Welsh**
Illustrator **Gary Hallgren, Max Ginsburg**
Publisher **Murdoch Magazines, Inc.**
Category **Story Presentation**
Date **October 6, 1986**

THE NEW
INTERIORS
CITY CHIC

BY MARILYN BETHANY

Every moviegoer the world over knows exactly how New Yorkers live:
Bachelors sleep under mirrored ceilings in round beds, kids just starting out make
do with orange crates in adorably cramped studios, and the dressed-for-dinner set
loll on satin sofas in penthouses. Clearly, it's time to update these stale stereo-
types, with fresher images that set new standards for city chic.

PHOTOGRAPHED BY OBERTO GILI

190

THE
BACHELOR
FLAT

OLD STYLE: BLACK, RED, AND READIER.

NEW STYLE As it happens, real men like lavender. And pink. And aqua. And all
those great Benjamin Moore golden yellows. When Carl Bernstein, of Watergate
fame, moved into this East Side apartment, he was dismayed by its lack of architectural interest. So he turned to his friend Chip Brawn, the artist, who transformed the
busy rooms with an abstract application of paint.

190A

THE
LOFT

OLD STYLE: MYSTIC OF RESIDENCE.

NEW STYLE When interior designer Peter P.
Carlson moved into an 18-by-40-foot former
tango parlor in Little Italy, the first thing he did
was replace the metal-framed windows with
six-over-six wood ones. "I had just moved from
a classic loft—huge windows, bright light, bare
floor, floating kitchen. It was like living in the
middle of an industrial park." In the new place,
he's struck a more conventional, residential
pose without losing the best of loft life— "being
able to walk without bumping into things."

190B

75

190
Publication **New York**
Art Director **Robert Best**
Designer **Josh Gosfield, Betsy Welsh**
Photographer **Oberto Gili**
Publisher **Murdoch Magazines, Inc.**
Category **Story Presentation**
Date **September 22, 1986**

Progressive Architecture

Rafael Moneo

With this article, P A introduces to its
readers Madrid architect Rafael Moneo, now
Chairman of the Architecture Department at
Harvard's Graduate School of Design.
On the next pages, Moneo's recently
completed National Museum of Roman Art
in Merida, Spain, is shown. Following the
museum is coverage of two earlier buildings
by Moneo. Also included are comments from
an interview of Moneo by P A editors (p. 78).

191

191A

191B

191
Publication **Progressive Architecture**
Art Director **Richelle J. Huff**
Designer **Samuel G. Shelton**
Photographer **Luis Casals, Diede von Schaewen**
Publisher **Penton Publishing Co.**
Category **Story Presentation**
Date **June 1986**

Progressive Architecture

Interior Design
The State of the Art

ARCHITECTURE and interior design haven't had a really good philosophical crisis in a decade. So does this mean that interiors have become predictable or boring? Hardly. We may not witness the birth of a new language of architecture every week, but that's because we're too busy trying to understand the old ones. One of Post-Modernism's most valuable—and least understood—lessons is that are revolution, no matter how glorious, can degenerate into lockstep repression. That was why so many architects and designers abandoned Modernism, and it is also why they're questioning copycat historicism in the search for an intelligent synthesis of past and present.

The projects (and people) featured in this year's interiors issue embody this goal. We begin with a group of projects from the West Coast, which in the last few years has emerged as a breeding ground for new ideas. The region's do-your-own-thing liberalism is a source of amusement to many Easterners) has, in fact, fostered offbeat, original approaches to theory (the art/architecture crossover evident in Peter Shire's house or A2Z's offices, both in Los Angeles, and the fast-food shop by Tom Grondona in San Diego), and a real inventiveness in the use of humble materials (as in the warehouse renovations by Schweitzer-Kellen's City Restaurant in Los Angeles, and in Anderson/Schwartz's offices for Windham Hill Productions in Palo Alto (ironically, it took a New York firm to bring Gehry's ideas to the conservative Bay Area). Most of these projects are small but highly visible, with clients who tend to be young entrepreneurs who are willing to take as much of a risk on design as there are in their businesses. And, instead of apologizing for relatively small budgets, their architects and designers are genuinely engaged by the problem of making more out of less.

The issue of economy of means—not so much economic as formal—arises in our two interior design profiles, which are intended to place design projects in a broader context, and which we plan to do more often. Jiřrina Kerr Associates has successfully synthesized 20th Century influences into a distinctive vocabulary that has transformed the London retail scene. Haigh Space comes out of a similarly Modernist tradition that is sharpened by a playfully contemporary sensibility, to ensure that everything from a warehouse renovation to a mass-produced chair combines pragmatic functionalism with wit and style.

Of the remaining projects, Gwathmey Siegel's restrained remodeling of Knoll International's Chicago showroom reflects showroom design's current conservation after a period of freewheeling experimentation. Susana Torre with Wank Adams Slavin Architects demonstrates the power of conceptual rigor in her renovation of Columbia University's Schermerhorn Hall. And, finally, we offer a reminder that architects were tinkering with Classicism long before the words "post" and "Modern" ever shared a hyphen: the Philadelphia Museum of Art's restoration of a room designed by Robert Adam for the now-demolished Lansdowne House in London.

The skeptics among us might say that "eclecticism" is simply a euphemism for "confusion." But eclecticism, for better or worse, is the state of the art today. The projects shown on the following pages represent varied modes of expression, but their designers all believe that there need be no mutual exclusivity between function and art, or between economy and eloquence. No confusion there.
Pilar Viladas

192

Table Setting

In transforming an old carpet warehouse into a new home for a successful restaurant, Schweitzer-Kellen Architects knew that underdone was better than overcooked.

192A

All 4 One

A self-described "collaborative argument" among art, architecture, and design, A2Z combined the eclectic interests of their three partners with a hands-on approach to create an office that doubles as the young firm's own best advertisement.

192B

192
Publication **Progressive Architecture**
Art Director **Richelle J. Huff**
Designer **Richelle J. Huff**
Agency **Hawthorne/Wolfe Design**
Photographer **Tim Street-Porter**
Publisher **Penton Publishing Co.**
Category **Story Presentation**
Date **September 1986**

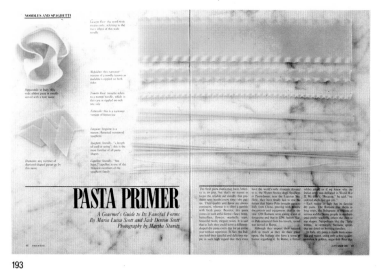

PASTA PRIMER

A Gourmet's Guide to Its Fanciful Forms
By Maria Luisa Scott and Jack Denton Scott
Photography by Martha Stanitz

193

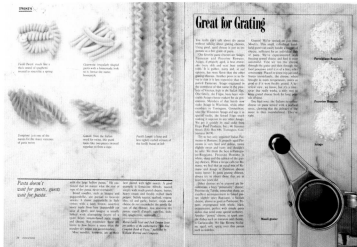

Great for Grating

Pasta doesn't wait for guests, guests wait for pasta.

193B

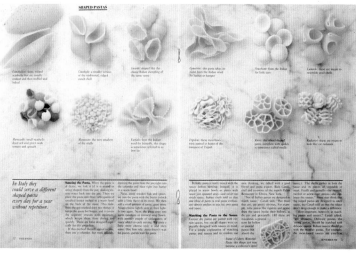

In Italy they could serve a different shaped pasta every day for a year without repetition.

78

193A

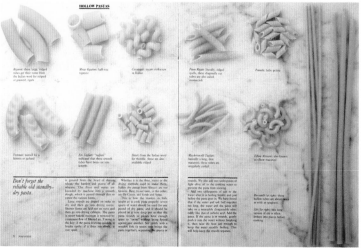

Don't forget the reliable old standby— dry pasta.

193C

193
Publication **Food & Wine**
Art Director **Will Hopkins, Ira Friedlander**
Photographer **Martha Stanitz**
Publisher **American Express Publishing Co.**
Category **Story Presentation**
Date **September 1986**

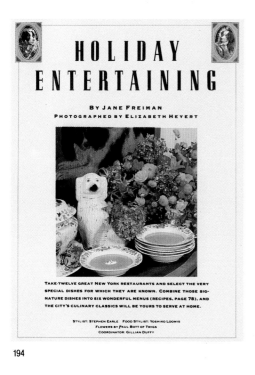

HOLIDAY ENTERTAINING

BY JANE FREIMAN
PHOTOGRAPHED BY ELIZABETH HEYERT

TAKE TWELVE GREAT NEW YORK RESTAURANTS AND SELECT THE VERY SPECIAL DISHES FOR WHICH THEY ARE KNOWN. COMBINE THOSE SIGNATURE DISHES INTO SIX WONDERFUL MENUS (RECIPES, PAGE 78), AND THE CITY'S CULINARY CLASSICS WILL BE YOURS TO SERVE AT HOME.

STYLIST: STEPHEN EARLE   FOOD STYLIST: YOSHIKO LOOMIS
FLOWERS BY PAUL BOTT OF TWIGS
COORDINATOR: GILLIAN DUFFY

194

STAR FISH

IF YOU DO IT RIGHT—AND IT CAN BE DONE EVEN IN THE SMALLEST NEW YORK APARTMENT—GUESTS SHOULD ARRIVE IN BLACK TIE FOR THIS GLAMOROUS LITTLE DINNER THAT IS LAVISH YET STILL VERY LIGHT. HERE ARE TWO STELLAR—AND SURPRISINGLY EASY—DISHES FROM LE BERNARDIN'S DASHING YOUNG FRENCH CHEF, GILBERT LE COZE. HIS INTENSE TRUFFLE-INFUSED OYSTERS BATHED IN WARM HERBED VINAIGRETTE ARE SHOWSTOPPERS. ADD SUBLIME SWEETWATER PRAWNS (A NEWLY IMPORTED CARIBBEAN CRUSTACEAN) FROM CHANTERELLE'S CHEF, DAVID WALTUCK, AND DINNER BECOMES AN AFFAIR TO REMEMBER.

SEAFOOD GALA FOR 6
RILLETTES OF SALMON
OYSTERS WITH TRUFFLES (LE BERNARDIN)
PRAWNS WITH GINGER-AND-LIME BUTTER (CHANTERELLE)
POACHED HALIBUT WITH WARM VINAIGRETTE
(LE BERNARDIN)
GRAND MARNIER SOUFFLE

194A

TAVOLA RUSTICANA

A ROMANTIC WINE CELLAR IS NOT A NECESSITY FOR CREATING A WONDERFULLY RUSTIC ITALIAN DINNER: THE AURA OF ABBONDANZA THAT SUFFUSES ITALIAN HOSPITALITY SEEMS IMPLICIT IN THIS MEAL. ERMINIA'S HOT-MOZZARELLA APPETIZER MARRIES FRESHLY MADE CHEESE WITH GARLIC-SCENTED TOMATOES AND RED PEPPERS. THE CENTERPIECE OF THE MEAL IS PRIMAVERA'S CELEBRATED ROSEMARY-SCENTED GRILLED BABY GOAT. ALSO FROM PRIMAVERA PADRONE NICOLA CIVETTA COMES THE JUSTLY FAMOUS TIRAMI SU, WHICH TRANSLATES AS "LIFT ME UP"—AND WILL DO JUST THAT, ITALIAN-STYLE.

RUSTIC ITALIAN DINNER FOR 12
HOT MOZZARELLA WITH TOMATOES AND RED PEPPERS (ERMINIA)
PASTA WITH GARLIC AND BROCOLETTI DI RAPE
GRILLED BABY GOAT (PRIMAVERA)
TIRAMI SU WITH COLD ZABAGLIONE (PRIMAVERA)

79

194B

FIRE AND SPICE

CHILL THE BEER, MIX THE MARGARITAS, AND SLICE FRUIT FOR SANGRIA. EVEN YOUR FRIENDS FROM TEXAS WILL HOOT AND HOLLER OVER THIS BUFFET, BECAUSE NO ONE CAN RESIST ROSA MEXICANO'S PERFECT GUACAMOLE, SPICED WITH FRESH HOT PEPPERS AND CILANTRO. SPREAD YOUR BEST INDIAN BLANKET ON THE TABLE. ORDER DOZENS OF FRESH CORN AND FLOUR TORTILLAS FROM TACAPULCO, AND PLOP THEM INTO A BASKET. THEN SET THE TORTILLAS ALONGSIDE THE FABULOUS, CRUNCHY CHILI-RUBBED CHICKEN AND RICH CORN RAGOUT FROM ARIZONA 206'S YOUNG, INVENTIVE CHEF, BRENDAN WALSH. BAKING YOUR FAVORITE FLAN FOR DESSERT IS ALL THAT'S LEFT TO DO.

SOUTHWESTERN BUFFET FOR 16
GUACAMOLE (ROSA MEXICANO)
SALSA VERDE AND PICO DE GALLO TORTILLA CHIPS
CHILI-RUBBED CHICKEN AND CORN RAGOUT
(ARIZONA 206)
FRESH CORN AND FLOUR TORTILLAS
FLAN WITH COCONUT TUILES

194C

194
Publication **New York**
Art Director **Robert Best**
Designer **Josh Gosfield, Betsy Welsh**
Photo Editor **Jordan Schaps**
Photographer **Elizabeth Heyert**
Publisher **Murdoch Magazines, Inc.**
Category **Story Presentation**
Date **October 27, 1986**

THE IRISH HUNT

OVER SLURRIED DITCHES,
HAIRY BANKS, AND FORMIDABLE STONE
WALLS, THEY RIDE TO HOUNDS WITH
UNMATCHED DERRING-DO.

195

BATH For a weekend away, smart Londoners choose Britain's secret cultural capital.

BY NICHOLAS SHRADY   PHOTOGRAPHS BY RICHARD DAVIES

196

195A

196A

195B

POCKETS OF MOMEN-TOUSNESS OPEN IN THE COURSE OF A ROUTINE WINTER DAY.

· Picking Up the Pace ·

196B

195
Publication **European Travel & Life**
Art Director **Jeanne Dzienciol**
Designer **Alejandro Gonzalez**
Photographer **Jean-Michel Voge**
Publisher **Murdoch Magazines, Inc.**
Category **Story Presentation**
Date **November/December 1986**

196
Publication **European Travel & Life**
Art Director **Jeanne Dzienciol**
Designer **Jeanne Dzienciol**
Photographer **Richard Davies**
Publisher **Murdoch Magazines, Inc.**
Category **Story Presentation**
Date **July/August 1986**

The Spirit of Sauna

IN FINLAND, WHERE THIS BATHING RITUAL WAS INVENTED CENTURIES AGO, THE PRACTICE IS STILL PURE AND SIMPLE

BY ELIZABETH GAYNOR

PHOTOGRAPHS BY KARI HAAVISTO

197

197A

81

197B

197
Publication **European Travel & Life**
Art Director **Jeanne Dzienciol**
Designer **Jeanne Dzienciol**
Photographer **Kari Haavisto**
Publisher **Murdoch Magazines, Inc.**
Category **Story Presentation**
Date **November/December 1986**

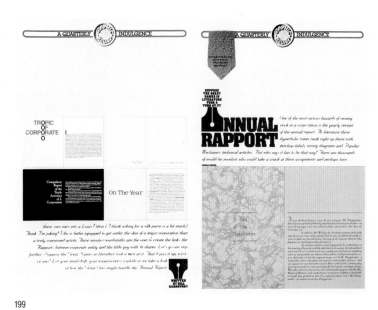

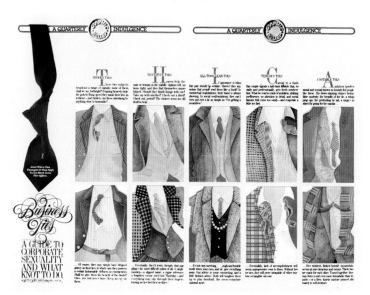

199
Publication **Graphic Relief**
Art Director **David Brier**
Designer **David Brier**
Photographer **Brien Graziano**
Category **Story Presentation**
Date **May 1986**

198
Publication **Team Talk**
Art Director **Douglas Wolfe**
Designer **Buck Smith**
Agency **Hawthorne/Wolfe Design**
Category **Story Presentation**
Date **December 1986**

200
Publication **Graphic Relief**
Art Director **David Brier**
Designer **David Brier**
Illustrator **Nina Winter**
Category **Story Presentation**
Date **May 1986**

201

201A

201
Publication **This People**
Art Director **Ron Stucki**
Designer **Ron Stucki**
Illustrator **Ron Stucki**
Category **Story Presentation**
Date **February/March 1986**

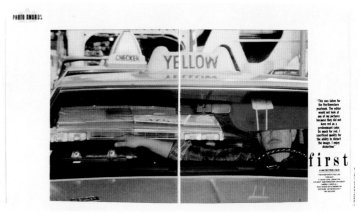

202A

202B

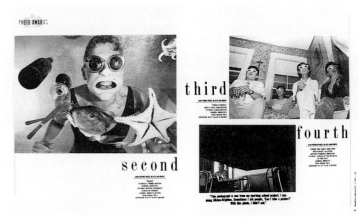

202C

202
Publication **The Boston Globe**
Art Director **Lynn Staley**
Designer **Lynn Staley**
Illustrator **Javier Romero**
Publisher **The Boston Globe**
Category **Story Presentation**
Date **October 12, 1986**

202

CONNOISSEUR

THE WALL

AND OTHER BIZARRE AFFLICTIONS PERTAINING TO BOSTON'S CRYPTO-MYTHICAL RED SOX

BY PHIL PATTON PHOTOGRAPHS BY JOHN KENNARD

203

203A

203B

85

203
Publication **Connoisseur**
Art Director **Carla Barr**
Designer **Stephanie Phelan**
Photographer **John Kennard**
Publisher **The Hearst Corporation**
Category **Story Presentation**
Date **September 1986**

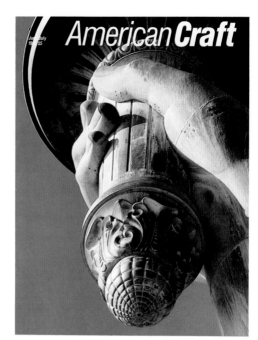

204

"I Lift My Lamp…"

This July Americans salute a great national symbol, the Statue of Liberty, resplendent in New York Harbor after a two-year restoration. More than 300 feet above the water, Liberty's torch is golden in the day's light, completely rebuilt by a 10-man team of specialists in repoussé from the Métalliers Champenois in Reims. As with Liberty's original construction, the roots of the current restoration lay in France.

204A

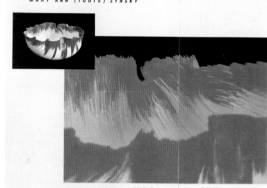

MARY ANN (TOOTS) ZYNSKY

PORTFOLIO

204B

204
Publication **American Craft**
Art Director **Kiyoshi Kanai**
Designer **Andrea Wollensak**
Photographer **Dan Cornish/ESTO,
Andrew Dean Powell**
Publisher **American Craft Council**
Category **Redesign**
Date **June/July 1986**

Liberty
Lifts Her Lamp Once More

By ALICE J. HALL ASSISTANT EDITOR

At once the world's largest metal statue, a tangible pledge of French-American friendship, and a beacon to immigrants, the great lady rising from New York Harbor is much more. In one stunning image recognized around the world, the Statue of Liberty says America. And in this country that so often places its celebrities on a pedestal, citizens have over the years taken Liberty from her lofty perch and into their hearts. That feeling of familial affection was evident among the workers putting up the scaffolding for much needed restoration in anticipation of the statue's 100th anniversary. Tony Soraci (right) summed up their accord, "It's a historic job, something to tell my grandchildren."

Likewise, the improbable tale of the statue's birth is something to remember and pass on. She was conceived by French intellectuals during after-dinner conversation near Paris in 1865. Chafing under the despotic rule of Napoleon III, host Édouard René Lefebvre de Laboulaye proposed a monument to American independence that French men and arms had helped achieve. It would be a gift of the French people for America's Centennial in 1876 and would reinforce ideals of equality and liberty still held by many Frenchmen. One guest, 31-year-old sculptor Frédéric-Auguste Bartholdi, began to plan a design. In 1871 he traveled the United States from coast to coast and spotted Bedloe's Island in New York Harbor: "Here . . . my statue must rise; here where people get their first view of the New World." He would spend the next 15 years turning idea into reality. —

205

The sonnet that is synonymous with the statue was penned by an American literary figure to help raise funds for the pedestal. "Give me your tired, your poor, your huddled masses yearning to breathe free," wrote Emma Lazarus (above), identifying the statue not as a classical goddess but as "Mother of Exiles." Her poem was included with works by Walt Whitman, Mark Twain, and Bret Harte in a portfolio auctioned for $1,500 at an art exhibit in December 1883.

Daughter of a wealthy New York merchant and member of an elite Sephardic Jewish community, Lazarus had been exposed to the effects of persecution when she met Jewish refugees fleeing the pogroms that swept Russia after the assassination of Tsar Alexander II in 1881. Thereafter she took up the cause of "the oppression of men and women by men and women" everywhere. But her poem slipped into obscurity despite James Russell Lowell's compliment: "I liked your sonnet . . . better than I like the Statue itself. . . . [It] gives its subject a raison d'être."

Still the pedestal fund languished, until a prominent publisher turned his newspaper into a fund-raiser. Joseph Pulitzer, who had himself come to America as a penniless Hungarian immigrant, put the statue's image in the logo of his New York World and used the paper's pages to shame New Yorkers for accepting "this splendid gift without our having provided even so much as a landing place for it." Appealing to "the people," he wrote, "let us not wait for the millionaires." By publishing the name of every donor in 1885, regardless of the size of the contribution, he raised $100,000 toward the $250,000 cost in five months, and pedestal construction moved forward.

In the years that followed, hundreds of immigrant ships entered New York Harbor, usually landing first- and second-class passengers in Manhattan and carrying third-class arrivals (right) to an immigration station at Ellis Island. For many, their first glimpse of America was the statue. "She was beautiful with the early morning light," one noted. "Everybody was crying. The whole boat bent toward her because everybody went out." Another recalled a "feeling among many of us that isn't it strange that here we are coming to a country where there is complete equality, but not quite so for the newly arrived immigrants. So third-class passengers had to come to Ellis Island."

In 1903 Emma Lazarus's poem was placed on a plaque inside the pedestal by a friend as a memorial to her, but not until the late 1930s did the sonnet move into the mainstream of American consciousness. By then the statue was increasingly associated with the earlier wave of immigration.

Today the plaque bearing Emma Lazarus's poem holds a place of honor in the statue's museum. The main building at Ellis Island that processed more than 12 million arrivals between 1892 and 1954 is being renovated as a museum honoring the immigrants.

National Geographic, July 1986

205A

"Men, they've got Liberty in a cage," a youngster cried out at the disconcerting sight on television of the statue imprisoned by scaffolding. Last November 25, as a Coast Guard helicopter hovered (right), a crane hoisted the new torch into place, an event marking one of the last chapters in the three-and-a-half-year, 31-million-dollar renovation. It began with an inch-by-inch inspection of the interior.

The worst problem were rust and corrosion. The statue had always leaked, and corrosion due to galvanic action occurred wherever iron ribs were held against the copper skin in copper fastenings, despite an insulating asbestos backing. Where the saddlelike fastenings had fallen off, river holes (below) exposed the interior to more moisture.

Supersized inside the two-foot-wide tablet, metalworker Mark Scola (left) removes one of the 1,800 corroded, paint-covered ribs. Each was replicated in a malleable rust-and-corrosion-resistant stainless steel known as 316L. Scola and Richard Santisi (lower left) used the old rib as a template for the new one, which they bent back with Teflon-coated tape to prevent rebanding on the skin side and to add insulation between the two metals.

During its earlier life the statue's interior was "improved" with tar...

...probably in an effort to keep out water, and painted at least seven times. Liquid nitrogen was applied to freeze and crack the paint; the tar came off with blasts of grit-softener bicarbonate, whose residue is seen above during the cleaning process. Stripped bare, the brown copper revealed the hammer marks of its creation.

National Geographic, July 1986

205B

205
Publication **National Geographic**
Art Director **Gerard A. Valerio**
Designer **Gerard A. Valerio**
Photographer **Various**
Publisher **The National Geographic Society**
Category **Story Presentation**
Date **July 1986**

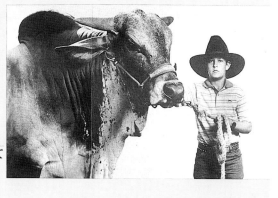

THE PARTINS:
THE NEXT GENERATION

•

PHOTOS BY GEORGE SKENE

Bo and the bull

Bo Tyson, 13, grandson of Couch Partin, with one of his grandfather's registered show bulls. "Wrinkled Horns 307," who weighs about as much as your average family car, but can be handled with ease by an experienced cowboy.

206A

Easy riders

They're working ranchers and representative of the fifth and fourth generation of Partins: Carlos Partin, 13; Davis Calderon, 19, both grandsons of Couch Partin; Earl Partin's son, Rex Partin, 33; and Couch's son, Mike Partin, 43.

On the fence

Roy F. Partin, 7, Ben Partin, 7, Ricky South, 8, and Brandy Tyson, 10, all have been in the horse before they began kindergarten. That's not unusual in their family; the children's parents, grandparents and great-grandparents did the same. But will this fifth generation of Partins go on to be cowboys? That remains to be seen, given family history, however, we'd bet on it.

At home on the range

He may look a native of the Australian outback, but Doug Partin, 42, was born and raised just south of Orlando. Doug, son of Dan Partin, played football at the University of Florida in the '60s, earned a degree in animal husbandry, then returned to the family ranch. He now manages a ranch near Kenansville and helps out on his father's ranch in his "spare" time.

206B

John boy

He's got two good reasons to chew tobacco: He's both a cowboy and a baseball player. John Partin, 23, represents what his grandmother, Mildred "Pattie" Partin, refers to as "our hope for the future of ranching." He attended Rollins College on a baseball scholarship, earned a degree in economics and has returned to work on the family ranch.

206

206
Publication **Florida Magazine**
Art Director **Santa Choplin**
Designer **Santa Choplin, Bill Henderson**
Photographer **George Skene**
Publisher **Sentinel Communications Co.**
Category **Story Presentation**
Date **November 23, 1986**

207

208

207A

208A

89

207B

207
Publication **The New York Times Magazine**
Art Director **Ken Kendrick, Diana LaGuardia**
Designer **Ken Kendrick**
Photographer **Letizia Battaglia, Franco Zecchin**
Publisher **The New York Times**
Category **Story Presentation**
Date **May 18, 1986**

208
Publication **The New York Times Magazine**
Art Director **Diana LaGuardia**
Designer **Kevin McPhee**
Photographer **Sebastiao Salgado**
Publisher **The New York Times**
Category **Story Presentation**
Date **September 7, 1986**

Once they were many; now they are so few. Nearly three and a half million Jews lived in Poland in 1939, and their homes, synagogues, and schools throbbed with an exuberance that made Poland a center of world Jewish culture. Then came the Holocaust...

In the years since, anti-Semitism has driven thousands more from Poland. Today the remaining Jews number perhaps 5,000, nearly all of them old, scattered like withered straw across the Polish plain.

Sara and Rafael Adar (right) live in Włodawa, on the Soviet border. Sara was a high-spirited young woman when the Germans marched into town; she swam the river bordering her family's farm and fled to the Soviet side. Seven years later she returned to find she had no family. Rafael too lost everyone. They met and married after the war. Now their world, once vibrant with Jewish life, is quiet. "We are making our exit," say the old Jews. "We will be gone in a minute."

Other survivors bear death-camp tattoos and grim memories. Few want anything to do with strangers. Photographer Tomasz Tomaszewski and author Małgorzata Niezabitowska, a husband-and-wife team, worked for years to build the trust implicit in the following story.

—THE EDITOR

REMNANTS: *The Last Jews of Poland*

By MAŁGORZATA NIEZABITOWSKA   Photographs by TOMASZ TOMASZEWSKI

363

384

National Geographic, September 1986

The Last Jews of Poland

385

366

209
Publication **National Geographic**
Art Director **Robert W. Madden**
Designer **Robert W. Madden**
Photographer **Tomasz Tomaszewski**
Publisher **The National Geographic Society**
Category **Story Presentation**
Date **September 1986**

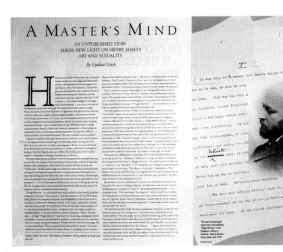

A MASTER'S MIND

AN UNPUBLISHED STORY
SHEDS NEW LIGHT ON HENRY JAMES'S
ART AND SEXUALITY

By Cynthia Ozick

210A

HUGH
MERROW

By Henry James

210
Publication **The New York Times Magazine**
Art Director **Diana LaGuardia**
Designer **Audrey Razgaitis**
Illustrator **Harvey Dinnerstein**
Publisher **The New York Times**
Category **Story Presentation**
Date **October 26, 1986**

211

211A

211B

211
Publication **Dallas Life Magazine**
Art Director **Lesley Becker**
Designer **Lesley Becker**
Photographer **William Snyder,
Patricia Franceschin**
Publisher **Dallas Morning News**
Category **Story Presentation**
Date **September 7, 1986**

212

212A

212B

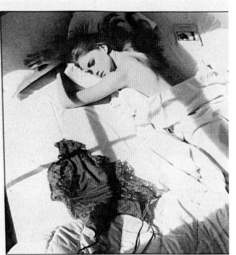

212C

212
Publication**Daily News Magazine**
Art Director **Janet Froelich**
Illustrator **Bob Murray**
Photographer **Hand tinting by West Murray**
Publisher **The Tribune Co.**
Category **Story Presentation**
Date **November 30, 1986**

Beauty/Fashion

THE POWER OF ARTIFICE

BY ANNE HOLLANDER

There has always been a mystical interplay between beauty and fashion. But it is the face that must go with everything. This fall, hand-in-hand with a return to femininity in clothes, there is a new drama in makeup and hair.

213

PARIS COUTURIERS, EMPLOYING THE SERVICES OF MASTER MAKEUP ARTISTS AND HAIR STYLISTS, HIGHLIGHTED THEIR COLLECTIONS WITH DRAMATIC AND DIFFERENT EFFECTS.

94

213A

AUTUMN IN PARIS

BY MARIAH McEVOY

213B

Fashion Preview
BY PATRICIA McCOLL

PARIS
SELF-CONFIDENT CLOTHES FOR SPRING

Two attitudes, caution and creativity, mark the Paris mood.

214

214A

214B

213
Publication **The New York Times Magazine**
Art Director **Diana LaGuardia**
Designer **Kevin McPhee**
Photographer **Wilfrid Rouff, Marc Bulka, Michael Geiger, Alexander Ager**
Publisher **The New York Times**
Category **Story Presentation**
Date **September 21, 1986**

214
Publication **The New York Times Magazine**
Art Director **Diana LaGuardia**
Designer **Audrey Razgaitis**
Photographer **Michel Compte**
Publisher **The New York Times**
Category **Story Presentation**
Date **October 12, 1986**

215

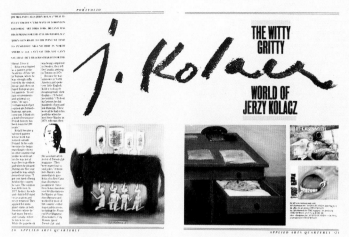

216

215A

216A

95

215
Publication **Applied Arts Quarterly**
Art Director **George Haroutiun, Bonita Collins**
Designer **George Haroutiun, Bonita Collins**
Photographer **Michael Pilon**
Publisher **Applied Arts, Inc.**
Category **Story Presentation**
Date **Spring 1986**

216
Publication **Applied Arts Quarterly**
Art Director **George Haroutiun, Bonita Collins**
Designer **George Haroutiun, Bonita Collins**
Illustrator **Jerzy Kolacz**
Publisher **Applied Arts, Inc.**
Category **Story Presentation**
Date **Summer 1986**

217

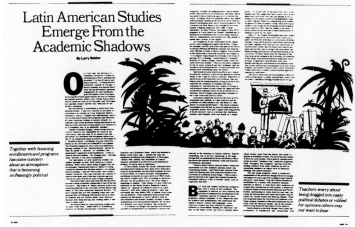

217A

217B

217
Publication **The New York Times—Education Life**
Art Director **Ron Couture**
Designer **Ron Couture**
Photographer **Various**
Publisher **The New York Times**
Category **Redesign**
Date **August 3, 1986**

218

218A

218B

218
Publication **W**
Art Director **Owen Hartley, Jean Griffin**
Designer **Edward Leida, Michael Liberatore**
Publisher **Fairchild Publications**
Category **Redesign**
Date **September 8, 1986**

The Hanimals, Humands and Humages of Mario Mariotti

When an artist is categorized as "conceptual," you had better be prepared for some surprises. Forget any notions you ever had of how a painting, a drawing, a piece of sculpture or a film should look. Conceptual art is an art of ideas. Sometimes the artist executes the concept completely. Sometimes it's enough to set an idea down on paper for others to contemplate...or execute if they please. But either way, the concepts are supposed to ignite the imagination and open new vistas. They have also been known to shock, mystify, frustrate, confuse, provoke, and captivate audiences with their unexpectedness.

Mario Mariotti of Florence, Italy is a contemporary artist who has worked in

219

219A

219C

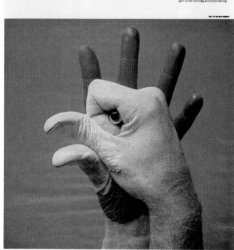

219B

219D

219
Publication **Upper & Lower Case**
Art Director **Bob Farber**
Designer **Bob Farber**
Illustrator **Mario Mariotti**
Photographer **Roberto Marchiori**
Publisher **International Typeface Corporation**
Category **Story Presentation**
Date **November 1986**

220

220A

220B

220
Publication **New York University Magazine**
Art Director **Steven Hoffman**
Designer **Steven Hoffman**
Illustrator **Alexa Grace**
Publisher **New York University**
Category **Format**
Date **Winter 1986**

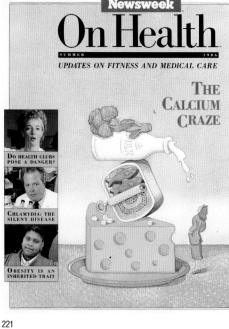

221

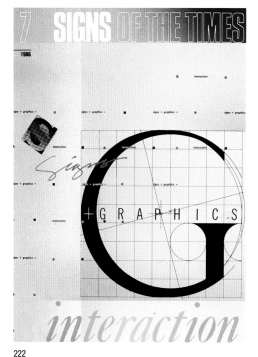

222

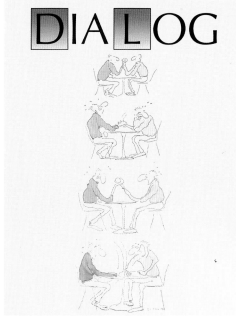

223

222A

100

221A

223A

221
Publication **Newsweek on Health**
Art Director **Steven Hoffman**
Designer **Steven Hoffman**
Illustrator **Mary Lynn Blasutta**
Publisher **Newsweek, Inc.**
Category **Format**
Date **Spring, Summer, Winter 1986**

222
Publication **Signs of the Times**
Art Director **Magno Relojo, Jr.**
Designer **Magno Relojo, Jr.**
Photo Editor **Alan Brown**
Photographer **Photo Design/Alan Brown**
Category **Format**
Date **December 1986**

223
Publication **Dialog**
Art Director **Wendy Edwards Lowitz**
Designer **Wendy Edwards Lowitz**
Illustrator **Linda Kelen**
Publisher **Abbott Laboratories**
Category **Format**
Date **January, March, May 1986**

224

225

226

224
Publication **Spy**
Art Director **Stephen Doyle**
Designer **Rosemarie Sohmer**
Illustrator **Rodrigo Shopis**
Photographer **Various**
Publisher **A/S/M Communications Co.**
Category **Format**
Date **October 1986**

225
Publication **Spy**
Art Director **Stephen Doyle**
Designer **Rosemarie Sohmer**
Photographer **Various**
Publisher **A/S/M Communications Co.**
Category **Format**
Date **October 1986**

226
Publication **Spy**
Art Director **Stephen Doyle**
Designer **Rosemarie Sohmer**
Photographer **Various**
Publisher **A/S/M Communications Co.**
Category **Format**
Date **November 1986**

227

227A

227B

102

227
Publication **Photo/Design**
Art Director **Deborah Lewis**
Designer **Deborah Lewis**
Photographer **Dennis Manarchy**
Publisher **Lakewood Publications**
Category **Format**
Date **May/June 1986**

228

228A

228B

228
Publication **ZapMail Images**
Art Director **Kevin B. Kuester,**
Madsen and Kuester, Inc.
Designer **Kevin B. Kuester**
Illustrator **Henry Martin**
Photographer **Arthur Mayerson**
Publisher **Federal Express Corporation**
Category **Format**
Date **February 1986**

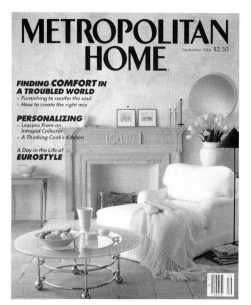

229

229A

229C

229B

229
Publication **Metropolitan Home**
Art Director **Don Morris**
Designer **Richard Ferretti**
Publisher **Meredith Corp.**
Category **Special/Single Issue**
Date **September 1986**

230

230A

230C

230B

105

230
Publication **Metropolitan Home**
Art Director **Don Morris**
Designer **Richard Ferretti**
Publisher **Meredith Corp.**
Category **Special/Single Issue**
Date **November 1986**

231

231A

231B

231
Publication **Metropolitan Home**
Art Director **Don Morris**
Designer **Richard Ferretti**
Publisher **The Meredith Corporation**
Category **Redesign**
Date **November 1986**

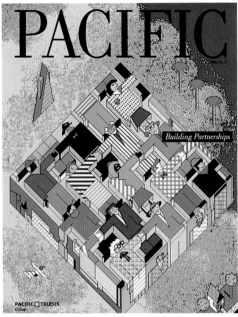

232

232A

Partners In The Common Interest

232B

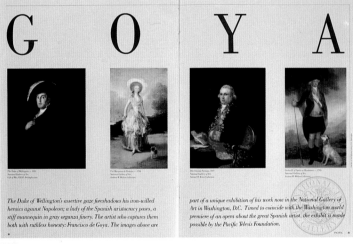

232C

232
Publication **Pacific**
Art Director **Michael Mabry**
Designer **Michael Mabry, Renee Holsen**
Illustration Editor **Teresa Ruano**
Publisher **Pacific Telesis Group**
Category **Redesign**
Date **December 1986**

233

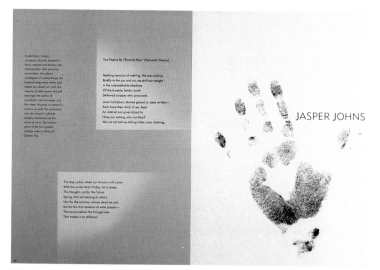

233A

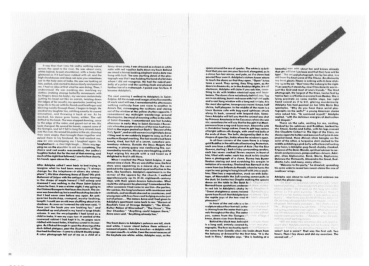

233B

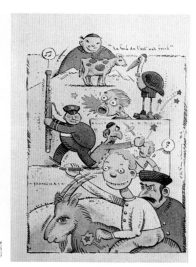

233C

233
Publication **Normal**
Art Director **Paul Davis**
Designer **Paul Davis**
Illustrator **Various**
Photographer **Various**
Publisher **Normal, Inc.**
Category **Special/Single Issue**
Date **1986**

234

234A

234B

234C

234
Publication **Nautical Quarterly**
Art Director **Clare Cunningham**
Designer **Clare Cunningham**
Photographer **Various**
Category **Special/Single Issue**
Date **Autumn 1986**

235

235A

235B

235C

110

235
Publication **Quality**
Art Director **Nora Sheehan, Mary K. Baumann**
Designer **Nora Sheehan, Mary K. Baumann**
Illustrator **Various**
Photographer **Various**
Publisher **Time, Inc.**
Category **Special/Single Issue**
Date **Winter 1987**

236

The
Ultimate
Grill

**The grill fire
is set with layers
of paper "pretzels,"
kindling and
charcoal.**

**Counterclockwise:
prawns, onion flower,
grilled red and yellow pepper,
baby corn, red onion, lamb
rolled in bacon, Japanese
eggplant, baby leeks,
adolescent zucchini flowers,
pork chop with rosemary,
patty pan squash.**

236A

A HOLLYWOOD STORY FROM

Rubicon Beach

FICTION BY STEVE ERICKSON

236B

111

236
Publication **L.A. Style**
Art Director **Rip Georges**
Publisher **L.A. Style, Inc.**
Category **Special/Single Issue**
Date **June 1986**

237

237A

237B

237C

237
Publication **New York**
Art Director **Robert Best**
Designer **Josh Gosfield, Betsy Welsh,**
Deborah Quintana
Illustrator **Various**
Photographer **Various**
Publisher **Murdoch Magazines, Inc.**
Category **Special/Single Issue**
Date **December 1, 1986**

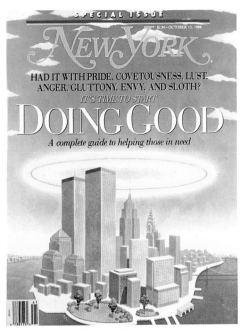

238

238A

238B

113

238
Publication **New York**
Art Director **Robert Best**
Designer **Josh Gosfield, Betsy Welsh**
Photo Editor **Susan Vermazen**
Publisher **Murdoch Magazines, Inc.**
Category **Special/Single Issue**
Date **October 13, 1986**

239A

239B

239

239C

239
Publication **New York**
Art Director **Robert Best**
Designer **Josh Gosfield, Betsy Welsh**
Photographer **Various**
Publisher **Murdoch Magazines, Inc.**
Category **Special/Single Issue**
Date **December 22–29, 1986**

240

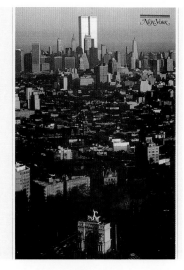

A NEW DAY DAWNS

BY PETE HAMILL

Brooklyn is hot, say the real-estate developers. Brooklyn is hip, say the writers and painters and musicians. Brooklyn is the true New York, say people who've lived there all their lives.

240A

ISLANDS IN THE CITY

BY PETER BLAUNER

Industrious West Indians have become one of the borough's great successes.

WILLIAM BABB
(TOP CENTER) AND
HIS FAMILY

115

A REVELER AT THE WEST INDIAN-AMERICAN DAY PARADE

240B

THE NEWEST LEFT BANK

BY AMY VIRSHUP

Brooklyn artists aren't addicted to flash and hype and instant success. All they need is light and space and quiet— and the ability to nurture their art until it's ready to show to the world.

THE ADAPTORS REHEARSE

240C

240
Publication **New York**
Art Director **Robert Best**
Designer **Josh Gosfield, David Walters**
Photo Editor **Jordan Schaps, Susan Vermazen**
Publisher **Murdoch Magazines, Inc.**
Category **Special/Single Issue**
Date **April 21, 1986**

241

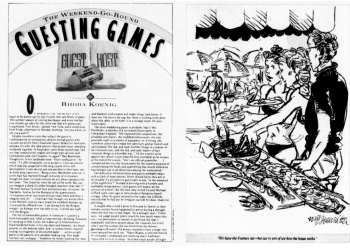

241A

241B

241C

241
Publication **New York**
Art Director **Robert Best**
Designer **Josh Gosfield, David Walters,**
Rhonda Rubinstein
Photographer **Various**
Publisher **Murdoch Magazines, Inc.**
Category **Special/Single Issue**
Date **June 30–July 7, 1986**

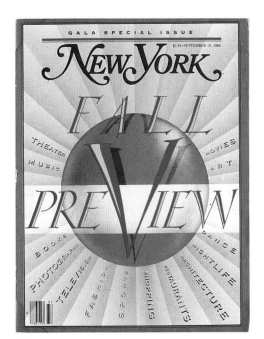

242

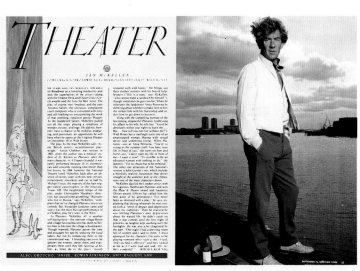

242A

242B

242C

242
Publication **New York**
Art Director **Robert Best**
Designer **Josh Gosfield, Betsy Welsh**
Photo Editor **Jordan Schaps, Susan Vermazen**
Illustrator **Paul Degan**
Photographer **Various**
Publisher **Murdoch Magazines, Inc.**
Category **Special/Single Issue**
Date **September 15, 1986**

243

243C

243
Publication **Time**
Art Director **Rudy Hoglund**
Designer **Tom Bentkowski**
Illustrator **Nick Fasciano**
Photographer **Roberto Brosan**
Publisher **Time, Inc.**
Category **Single Page/Spread**
Date **June 16, 1986**

244

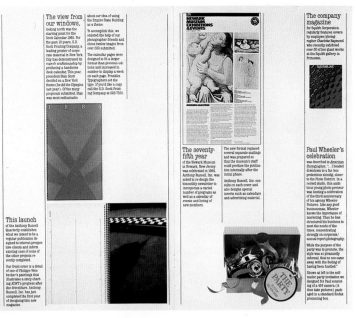

244A

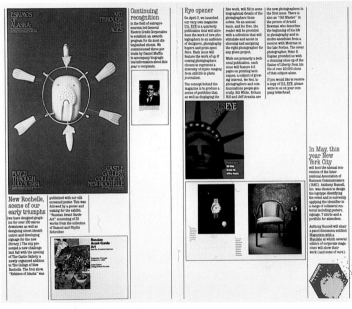

244B

119

244C

244
Publication **Anthony Russell Quarterly**
Art Director **Anthony Russell**
Designer **Casey Clark**
Publisher **Anthony Russell, Inc.**
Category **Overall**
Date **January 1986**

245

ANTHONY RUSSELL INC. NUMBER 3 APRIL 1986

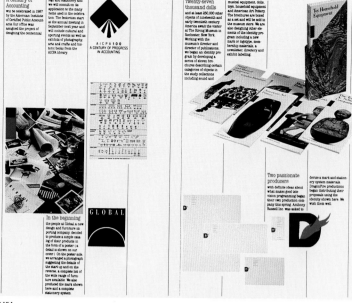

245A

245B

245C

245
Publication **Anthony Russell Quarterly**
Art Director **Anthony Russell**
Designer **Casey Clark**
Publisher **Anthony Russell, Inc.**
Category **Overall**
Date **April 1986**

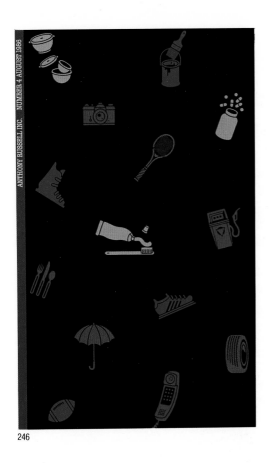

ANTHONY RUSSELL, INC.   NUMBER 4 AUGUST 1986

246

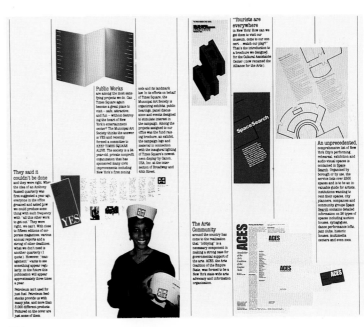

246A

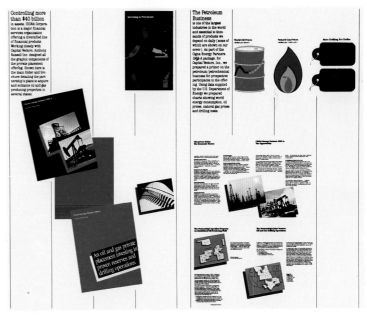

246B

246C

246
Publication **Anthony Russell Quarterly**
Art Director **Anthony Russell**
Designer **Casey Clark**
Publisher **Anthony Russell, Inc.**
Category **Overall**
Date **May 1986**

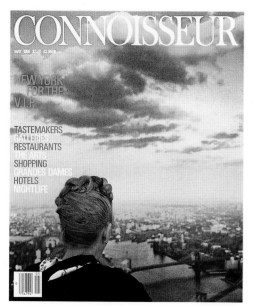

247

247A

247B

247C

247
Publication **Connoisseur**
Art Director **Carla Barr**
Designer **Carla Barr**
Photographer **Various**
Publisher **The Hearst Corporation**
Category **Special/Single Issue**
Date **May 1986**

248

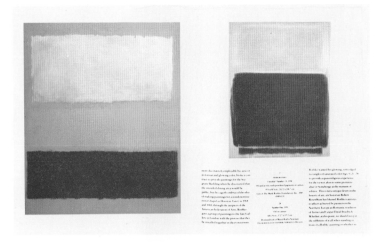

248A

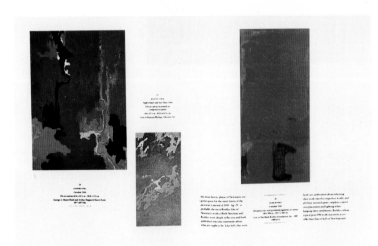

248B

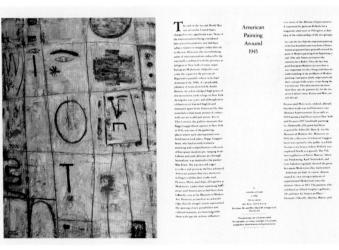

248C

248
Publication **Metropolitan Museum of Art Bulletin**
Art Director **Joan Holt**
Designer **Betty Binns**
Photographer **Various**
Publisher **Metropolitan Museum of Art**
Category **Special/Single Issue**
Date **December 15, 1986**

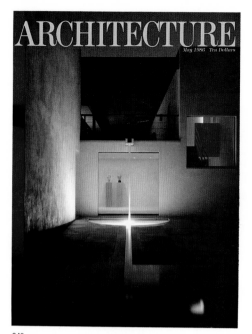

249

124

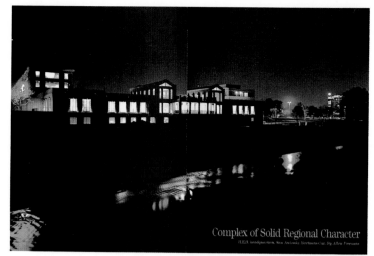

Complex of Solid Regional Character

H.E.B. headquarters, San Antonio. Architects Cox. By Allen Freeman.

249A

On Being Hip In Venice with Conviction

Project home. Venice Calif., Morpo & Rotondi (formerly Morphosis). By John Pastier.

249B

Contextual Tower Rises Above a '50s Classic

500 Park Tower, New York City. James Stewart Polshek & Partners. By Cervin Robinson.

249C

249
Publication **Architecture**
Art Director **Carole J. Palmer**
Publisher **The American Institute of Architects**
Category **Special/Single Issue**
Date **May 1986**

250

250A

250B

125

250C

250D

250
Publication **Progressive Architecture**
Art Director **Richelle J. Huff**
Designer **Richelle J. Huff**
Photographer **Ian Lambot**
Publisher **Penton Publishing Co.**
Category **Special/Single Issue**
Date **March 1986**

US EYE
NUMBER 2/WINTER 1986

Hans Neleman
Sandra Haber
Greg Murphey
Bruce Davidson
John Blaustein

251

Hans Neleman

Hans Neleman, 25, has had a circuitous, but relatively short, journey to a successful career in commercial photography. Born in Rotterdam, Neleman finished preparatory school in Holland, then enrolled at Goldsmiths University of London where he took a one year foundation course, sampling all the fine arts.

"Luckily, the last thing I did was photography," he says, "so I stuck with it. Originally I used photography as an impetus for painting and sculpture but ultimately I found it more immediate and appealing. I really don't have the patience for painting."

After completing a three-year degree in photography at The Polytechnic of Central London, (and being awarded "Photographer of the Year" by Kodak in Great Britain), Neleman moved to the United States in 1983, finishing a master's degree in studio art at New York University in one year.

He had done a good deal of editorial work in England and Europe while still a student so making the transition to New York was not so difficult, he says.

Neleman works mainly in large format for still life as well as fashion and portraiture. His favorite camera is an 8x10 Sinar which he describes as "the Rolls Royce of cameras." He also works occasionally as 2½x2½."

"I like the idea of rigidistic discipline of a large format camera," he says. "You really have to plan

and design the shot before you take it. It's not just a matter of running a lot of film through the camera and hoping you wind up with the right shot."

Neleman's career has begun to take off in New York and he's lately done work for CBS Records, Yves St. Laurent, Esquire, Art News, Manhattan Inc., Working Woman, and the Daily News Magazine, among others.

"The best thing about working in New York," Neleman says, "is that you're around talented people all the time. You have an opportunity to work with the best designers, editors and art directors. I find that's a tremendous inspiration for my own work."

 *(251A left photo)*

This assignment from Europe was to show the contrast between the New York East Village art scene and the uptown scene. This was done at the Patrick Fox Gallery. That's Patrick standing, with Robert Hawkins, one of his artists, kneeling. What I loved about the place was the texture and detail. I did this in 8x10 and with special camera movement was able to capture a wide angle look without much distortion.

This is a portrait of author C.D.B. Bryan, John O'Hara's step-son, taken in front of a gazebo at O'Hara's old residence in Connecticut. He's looking O'Hara's typewriter under his arm. I did the shot for Esquire, although they chose to use a still life of the typewriter by itself I photographed the same day.

251A

Sandra L. Haber

Sandra Haber, 29, is essentially a fine arts photographer whose montages—all done directly on film—have attracted an enthusiastic following among edit-multiphoto editors, particularly those at Esquire, Mademoiselle, and Manhattan, Inc. all of whom have given her assignments.

"I first started doing wire commercial work a couple of years ago and find a tremendous challenge," Haber says. "But basically, by training and temperament I'm a fine arts photographer."

Born in Sharon, Pa. Haber grew up in Youngstown, Ohio. She got a BFA in psychology after a dental College in Los Angeles, before going for an MFA in photography at the Rochester Institute of Technology.

Haber's work is represented in the permanent collections of such institutions as the Art Institute of Chicago, the International Museum of Photography in Rochester, the Los Angeles County Museum, the Oakland Museum, and the Museum of Modern Art in New York. Her most recent solo exhibition was at the Center for Contemporary

Arts in Santa Fe and the Center for Creative Photography in Taiwan.

"The style of the montages you see represented here just naturally evolved," she says. "I had been working with diptychs and triptychs and I began working this way about five years ago."

Haber composes on 2½" film, capturing all the elements on the negative, then printing the final result herself. In some cases, she has produced the right combination of elements for a successful montage in a half hour; others have taken two or three days to assemble. What she is going for, she says, is "the feeling of a place or a person, not a literal reading."

Although the results look rich, complex, and tricky to pull together, Haber says not much is left to chance. "I have a fairly good sense of how it's going to turn out," she says. "but once in a while there is a surprise on the negative. You can't control everything but that's part of the fun."

One of the things that has happened to me recently is that people ask me to do commissions. I did this for the parents of the kids in the photograph. We went to a swimming pool and they were really cute lunchbags so I traveled to photograph them that way rather than making them sit still.

This is a photograph I did while on assignment for Esquire at Coney Island. I was shooting for the summer travel issue and while I knew this wasn't really just able to fit that I was struck by the boys hanging around a round — calm and super-mixed bang it.

251B

This studio shot, against a colorful draped background, is striking because of the synchronized elegant poses by Carla Dunlap ("Pumping Iron") and Nancy Joffe, American Ballet Theatre. It was taken for an article about female muscles in New York Salt magazine.

This is a study of Gerald Pryor, head of the photography department at New York University, and one of my profile subjects. I partially positioned him in front of some of his work. I had achieved the same mood with the photograph as Pryor did with his work.

Bob Guralt, famous for his summer ads and Michael Jackson videos, is very busy these days but I was able to get him to look relaxed even though he was in the middle of a rush setting up. I did the picture for a Los Angeles magazine called Opera House.

251C

251
Publication **US Eye**
Art Director **Anthony Russell**
Designer **Casey Clark**
Publisher **US Eye Publishing**
Category **Special/Single Issue**
Date **Winter 1986**

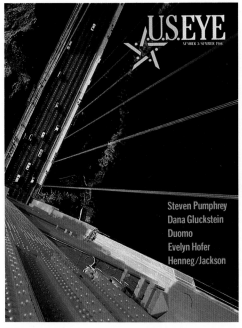

252

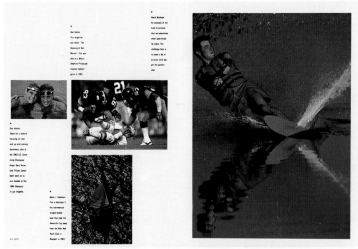

252A

252B

Masters:
Evelyn Hofer

252C

252
Publication **US Eye**
Art Director **Anthony Russell**
Designer **Casey Clark**
Publisher **US Eye Publishing**
Category **Special/Single Issue**
Date **August 1, 1986**

253

253A

253B

253C

253
Publication **The Boston Globe**
Art Director **Ronn Campisi**
Designer **Ronn Campisi**
Illustrator **Andrzej Dudzinski, Vivienne Flesher,**
Henrik Drescher
Publisher **The Boston Globe**
Category **Special Issue**
Date **October 6, 1986**

254

254A

254B

129

254C

254
Publication **The New York Times Magazine**
Art Director **Ellen Burnie**
Designer **Ellen Burnie**
Illustrator **Various**
Photographer **Jean Pagliusso**
Publisher **The New York Times**
Category **Special Issue**
Date **August 28, 1986**

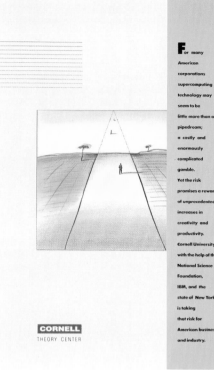

F or many American corporations supercomputing technology may seem to be little more than a pipedream; a costly and enormously complicated gamble. Yet the risk promises a reward of unprecedented increases in creativity and productivity. Cornell University, with the help of the National Science Foundation, IBM, and the state of New York, is taking that risk for American business and industry.

CORNELL THEORY CENTER

255

130

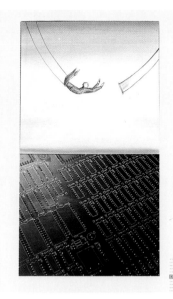

LEADING SCIENCE

AND INDUSTRY

INTO THE

SUPERCOMPUTER

AGE

255A

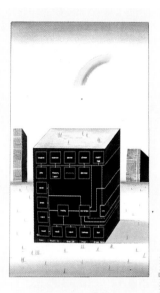

CORNELL THEORY CENTER

A TESTING GROUND FOR SUPERCOMPUTING TECHNIQUES AND APPLICATIONS IBM, Floating Point Systems, and Intel supercomputing equipment are up and running at Cornell. With support from the NSF and high-technology corporations, the Theory Center is expanding and upgrading multiple systems with state-of-the-art hardware. Scientists, engineers, and corporate associates have the opportunity to gain hands-on experience with a low-cost modular supercomputer and advanced graphics capabilities that promise to become the industry standard for the next century.

255B

CORNELL THEORY CENTER

A TESTING GROUND FOR THE NEXT GENERATION OF HARDWARE Cornell's vision of the future is parallel. Scientists at the Theory Center are working with two highly advanced parallel-processing systems based on architectures that are making possible almost unimaginable computing speeds. With the potential for hundreds, even thousands, of linked processors, these prototypes are a giant step toward the production-line for massively parallel machines. Leading computer manufacturers and scientists are testing hardware and developing information networks to meet future computing demands of unprecedented magnitude.

255C

255
Publication **Cornell Theory Center Brochure**
Art Director **Fausto Pellegrini**
Designer **Fausto Pellegrini, Nadia Pignatone**
Illustrator **Eugene Mihaesco**
Publisher **Cornell University**
Agency **Krukowski Associates**
Category **Special/Single Issue**
Date **1986**

A Different Breed of Ivy

History

Student Life

Admission

Costs

Location

Athletics

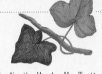

Applying to Binghamton

Financial Aid

Visiting the Campus

Undergraduate Majors and Concentrations

256A

De Ramis Antiquis
Novum Folium

(From Old Vines, a New Leaf)

IT GROWS ON THE WALLS of probably half of the colleges and universities in the United States, but it has come to symbolize qualities common to only a few. "Ivy" has long been synonymous with rigorous admissions standards, exceptional liberal arts education,

B I N G H A M T O N

256

131

256
Publication **Bulletin of the State University of New York at Binghamton**
Art Director **Fausto Pellegrini**
Designer **Nadia Pignatone**
Illustrator **Library of the Botanical Garden, NY**
Photographer **Various**
Publisher **State University of New York at Binghamton**
Agency **Krukowski Associates**
Category **Special/Single Issue**
Date **1986**

257

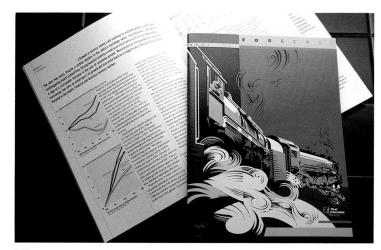

257A

257
Publication **First Interstate Bank Forecast,'86–'87**
Art Director **Ken White, Lisa Levin**
Designer **Petrula Vrontikis**
Illustrator **Don Weller**
Publisher **First Interstate Bancorp**
Category **Special/Single Issue**
Date **1986–87**

Genus Varium
Hederae

(A Different Breed of Ivy)

University Center at Binghamton

B U L L E T I N

State University of New York

258

W hen the State University of
New York at Binghamton was one
of only 17 universities named in a
recently published book, *The Public
Ivys,** we were skeptical at first.
Binghamton, like the distinguished
institutions with which it was grouped,

258A

258B

Professor or Partner?

258C

133

258
Publication **Bulletin of the State University of
New York at Binghamton**
Art Director **Fausto Pellegrini**
Designer **Nadia Pignatone**
Illustrator **Library of the Botanical Garden, NY**
Photographer **Various**
Publisher **State University of New York at Binghamton**
Agency **Krukowski Associates**
Category **Special/Single Issue**
Date **1986**

259

259B

259A

259C

259
Publication **Health Times**
Art Director **Fausto Pellegrini**
Designer **Giona Maiarelli**
Illustrator **Juan Suares Botas**
Publisher **St. Luke's-Roosevelt Hospital**
Agency **Krukowski Associates**
Category **Special/Single Issue**
Date **Summer 1986**

260

260A

260
Publication **Newman Design Associates**
Promotional Brochure
Art Director **Bob Newman**
Designer **Bob Newman**
Illustrator **Various**
Photographer **Various**
Publisher **Newman Design Associates, Inc.**
Agency **Newman Design Associates, Inc.**
Category **Special/Single Issue**
Date **August 1986**

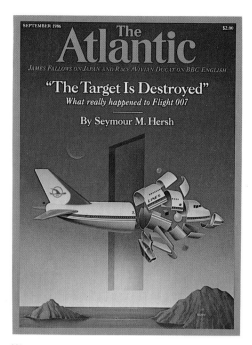

261

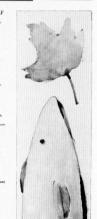

261A

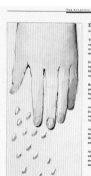

261B

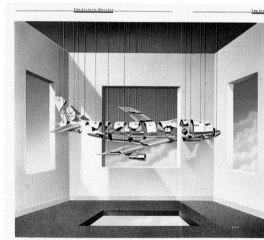

261C

261
Publication **The Atlantic Monthly**
Art Director **Judy Garlan**
Designer **Judy Garlan, Rhoda Gubernick**
Illustrator **Theo Rudnak**
Publisher **The Atlantic Monthly Co.**
Category **Overall**
Date **April, September, December 1986**

262

262A

262B

137

262C

262
Publication **Metropolitan Home**
Art Director **Don Morris**
Designer **Richard Ferretti**
Publisher **Meredith Corp.**
Category **Overall**
Date **September 1986**

263

263A

263B

263C

263
Publication **Connoisseur**
Art Director **Carla Barr**
Designer **Carla Barr**
Publisher **The Hearst Corporation**
Category **Overall**
Date **February, March, October 1986**

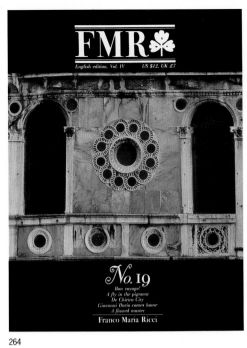

264

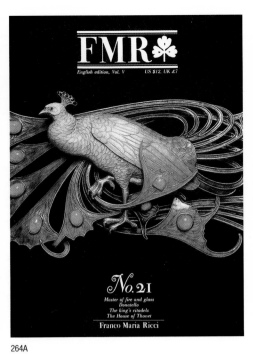

264A

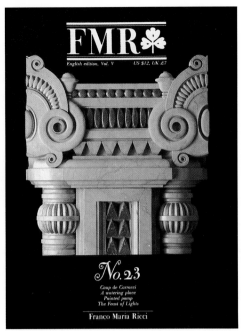

264B

264
Publication **FMR**
Art Director **Franco Maria Ricci**
Designer **Laura Casalis**
Publisher **FMR, Milan**
Category **Overall**
Date **April/May, August/September,
December 1986**

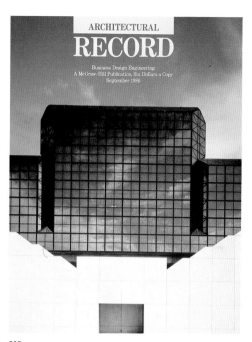

265

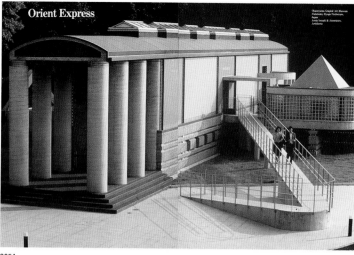

265A

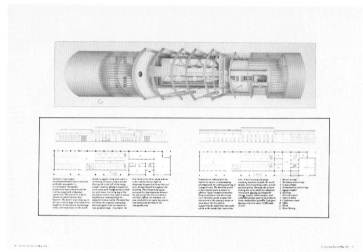

265B

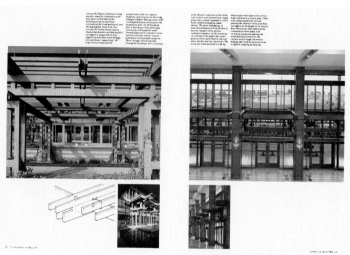

265C

140

266

266A

266B

266
Publication **Dallas Life Magazine**
Art Director **Lesley Becker**
Designer **Lesley Becker, Mary Jennings, Patrick Collins Mitchell**
Photographer **Lon Cooper, Ken Geiger, David Leeson, William Snyder, Laynie Morgan Lidji, Evans Caglage**
Publisher **Dallas Morning News**
Category **Entire Issues**
Date **March 16, August 31, November 23, 1986**

267

267A

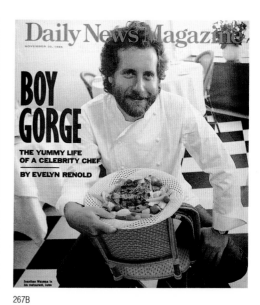

267B

268

267
Publication **Daily News Magazine**
Art Director **Janet Froelich**
Designer **Janet Froelich, Randy Dunbar,**
April Garston, Jodee Stringham
Publisher **The Tribune Co.**
Category **Entire Issues**
Date **September 7, October 19,**
November 30, 1986

268
Publication **Parade**
Art Director **Ira Yoffee, Chris Austopchuk**
Designer **Ira Yoffee, Chris Austopchuk**
Photographer **Deborah Feingold**
Publisher **Parade Magazine**
Category **Format**
Date **November 2, 1986**

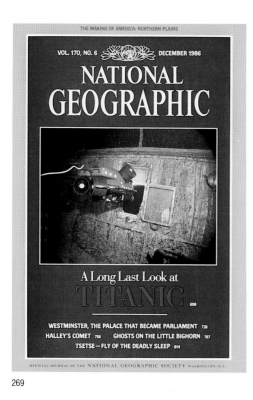

269

269A

269B

143

269C

269
Publication **National Geographic**
Art Director **Robert Madden**
Designer **Robert Madden, Gerard A. Valerio,**
Constance Phelps
Photographer **Various**
Publisher **The National Geographic Society**
Category **Overall**
Date **December 1986**

270

270A

270B

270C

144

270
Publication **W**
Art Director **Owen Hartley, Jean Griffin**
Designer **Michael Liberatore, Edward Leida**
Publisher **Fairchild Publications**
Category **Entire Issues**
Date **August 25, September 22,**
December 15, 1986

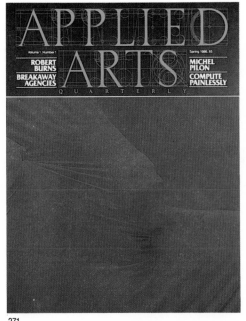

271

271A

271B

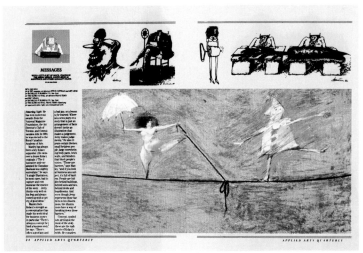

271C

271
Publication **Applied Arts Quarterly**
Art Director **George Haroutiun, Bonita Collins**
Designer **George Haroutiun, Bonita Collins**
Publisher **Applied Arts, Inc.**
Category **Overall**
Date **Fall 1986**

272

272A

272B

272C

272
Publication **Chili's, Inc. Annual Report**
Art Director **Brian Boyd**
Designer **Brian Boyd**
Photographer **Robert Latorre**
Publisher **Chili's, Inc.**
Agency **Richards Brock Miller Mitchell &**
Associates
Category **Special/Single Issue**
Date **1986 Annual Report**

273

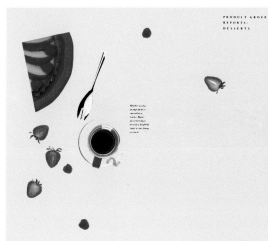

273A

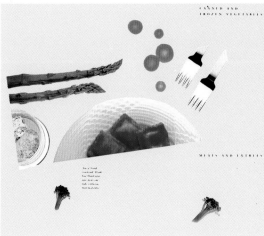

273B

273
Publication **Curtice-Burns Annual Report**
Art Director **Robert Meyer, Jean Page**
Designer **Jean Page**
Photographer **Joseph Chiu**
Publisher **Curtice-Burns, Inc.**
Agency **Robert Meyer Design**
Category **Special/Single Issue**
Date **1986 Annual Report**

274

274A

274B

274C

274

Publication **H.J. Heinz Annual Report**
Art Director **Bennett Robinson**
Designer **Bennett Robinson, Meera Singh**
Illustrator **John Berkey, Kinuko Craft,**
Malcolm T. Liepke, Julian Allen, Eraldo Carugati,
Max Ginsburg, James McMullan & others
Publisher **H.J. Heinz Co.**
Agency **Corporate Graphics, Inc.**
Category **Special/Single Issue**
Date **1986 Annual Report**

275

"Not only are people serving and enjoying fresh fruits and vegetables more than ever before, they are trying new and unusual varieties."

Kiwis, gooseberries, cherimoya, fiddlehead ferns, kumquats, white asparagus, kohlrabi, bok choy and oyster mushrooms are just a few of our fruits and vegetables from around the world.

REVIEW OF OPERATIONS

During the past year, we made dramatic progress in repositioning ourselves despite strong competition. Looking back over 1985, it is evident that better product quality, assortment, value and service have strengthened customer appeal and broadened our customer base. This upgrading has been carefully planned to strengthen Grand Union and Big Star's appeal in today's marketplace.

MERCHANDISING EFFORTS

Working women, higher educational levels, increased travel and more disposable income make today's consumer more demanding in terms of service, convenience and quality. All of these factors have impacted our merchandising strategy.

Responding to today's consumers' desire for more natural and healthful foods, a greater variety of foods, and more convenience foods, Grand Union has expanded the variety of products it carries and has introduced many new products and services which have influenced our customers' perception of us as the place to shop for quality, selection and value.

Research shows that the primary reason for selecting a supermarket is the quality and breadth of selection available in the produce department. In this area, Grand Union has positioned itself second to none. Buyers select only the best of each item being harvested at any given time anywhere in the world. Each item is selected must be flavorful, fresh and possess eye-appeal. Produce failing any one of these tests is not sold in our stores.

While much of our produce is obtained from Florida, California and the Northeast, as well as locally when in season, we also import produce which is either out-of-season or not available domestically. This gives added dimension to the produce program. We have developed our own product specifications, more rigid than those of the U.S. Department of Agriculture, and, if anywhere along the distribution system an item falls short of meeting these specifications, it is not placed on our shelves.

Responding to increased awareness of the many potentially harmful additives used in food handling and processing, we do not use sulfites to preserve freshness and we have greatly expanded our offering of natural and healthful foods. Sulfite-, sugar-free and all-natural products now claim an increasingly important portion of our product mix. Of particular interest is the introduction of natural beef into 300 stores. This beef, from medication-free cattle raised in a chemical-free environment without any artificial additives or growth stimulants in the feed, has been well received by our customers. In a period when beef consumption is declin-

275A

"Fresh fish and shellfish are the best fish and shellfish. If it's not fresh, it's not good enough for us to sell."

Red snapper, rock trout, wild mussels, steamers, whole Atlantic blue crab, clams in a basket, littleneck clams, flounder and squid.

future and complement our existing portfolio of traditional supermarkets.

Prototypes enable us to more precisely meet customer needs in each specific trade area, whether they are in the areas of produce, deli, bakery, meat, fresh fish or frozen food. Prototype specifications are constantly being upgraded as new ideas are successfully tested or as new, more efficient equipment becomes available.

Last year, we spent more than $46,000,000 in capital improvement programs designed primarily to strengthen our produce operations as well as some of our specialty departments.

As reported in the Chairman's Letter, $250 million has been allocated to capital improvement over the next three years with $75 million allotted for fiscal 1986 alone. We are especially targeting the New York, New Jersey, Vermont and Atlanta, Georgia, markets for development. In these areas, we have identified some 35 locations for future new store development. When reviewing last year's positive improvement on a store-by-store basis, the figures reveal larger increases in stores funded for capital improvement, proof that the prototype models are a success.

In addition to the company's commitment to develop new locations, a strong emphasis has been placed on upgrading existing stores within their present confines, many of which can also be expanded by 10,000 to 15,000 square feet at very favorable occupancy rates.

This aggressive capital improvement program will significantly improve the sales and profit potential of every store in our company.

TAKING OUR MESSAGE TO THE CUSTOMER

The right item at the right time in the right place at the right price — we've got it all. The challenge is to convey this message to millions of potential customers. In addition to standard methods of promotion — newspaper, radio, circulars and television — mostly item-price advertising, 1985 can us boldly forge in a new direction for the supermarket industry — image advertising. Everything about our stores says "hot" "new" "fresh" "natural." We have a powerful message to convey to millions of television viewers.

Continued use of Consumer Price Finder booklets reinforces our low price image, as does the Red Dot Price Finder for Specials.

Intensified use of in-ad funds provides high visibility for national brands and reinforces our national brand low price image.

Usually used to convey only item and price information, our in-store signage has been redesigned to provide more useful information. "New," "First of the Season" and "Locally Grown" are part some of the signs now being used to show customers we care.

275B

275
Publication **Grand Union Annual Report**
Art Director **Milton Glaser**
Designer **Milton Glaser, David Freedman**
Photographer **Matthew Klein**
Publisher **The Grand Union Co.**
Agency **Milton Glaser, Inc.**
Category **Special/Single Issue**
Date **1986 Annual Report**

276

276A

276B

276
Publication **Warner Communications, Inc.,**
Annual Report
Art Director **Peter Harrison**
Designer **Susan Hochbaum**
Illustrator **Sue Huntley, Donna Muir**
Photographer **Neal Slavin**
Publisher **Warner Communications, Inc.**
Agency **Pentagram Design**
Category **Special/Single Issue**
Date **1986 Annual Report**

277A

277

277
Publication **Datacopy Annual Report**
Art Director **Mark Anderson**
Designer **Earl Gee**
Photographer **Henrik Kam**
Publisher **Datacopy Corp.**
Category **Special/Single Issue**
Date **1986 Annual Report**

278

278A

278B

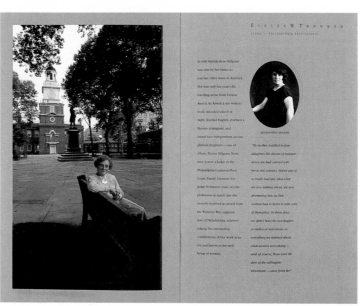

278C

278
Publication **Lomas & Nettleton Mortgage
Investors Annual Report**
Art Director **Steve Miller**
Designer **Steve Miller**
Photographer **Greg Booth**
Publisher **Lomas & Nettleton Mortgage Investors**
Agency **Steve Miller**
Category **Special/Single Issue**
Date **1986 Annual Report**

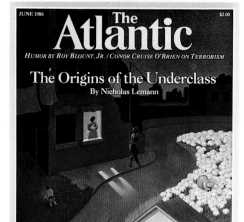

279

280

154

279
Publication **The Atlantic Monthly**
Art Director **Judy Garlan**
Designer **Judy Garlan**
Illustrator **Robert Goldstrom**
Publisher **The Atlantic Monthly**
Category **Cover**
Date **June 1986**

280
Publication **Print Magazine**
Art Director **Andrew P. Kner**
Designer **Bob Conge**
Illustrator **Bob Conge**
Publisher **RC Publications, Inc.**
Category **Cover**
Date **May/June 1986**

281

282

283

281
Publication **Playboy**
Art Director **Tom Staebler**
Designer **Kerig Pope**
Illustrator **Blair Drawson**
Publisher **Playboy Enterprises, Inc.**
Category **Single Page/Spread**
Date **June 1986**

282
Publication **Playboy**
Art Director **Tom Staebler**
Designer **Kerig Pope**
Illustrator **Blair Drawson**
Publisher **Playboy Enterprises, Inc.**
Category **Single Page/Spread**
Date **December 1986**

283
Publication **Playboy**
Art Director **Tom Staebler**
Designer **Kerig Pope**
Illustrator **Braldt Bralds**
Publisher **Playboy Enterprises, Inc.**
Category **Single Page/Spread**
Date **December 1986**

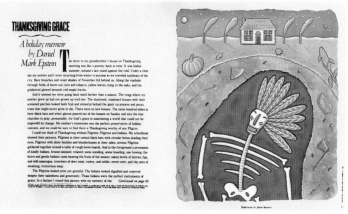

THANKSGIVING GRACE

*A holiday memoir
by Daniel
Mark Epstein*

284

¡Aleluya,
Hermano!

BY FRANCISCO AYALA

In this
classic short
story by one
of Spain's
most gifted
and prolific
writers, the
message is in
the music.
Translation by
Toby Talbot.

285

WHAT YOU SEE,
WHAT YOU GET

By KEVIN KELLY

286

284
Publication **The Boston Globe**
Art Director **Lynn Staley**
Designer **Lynn Staley**
Illustrator **Jamie Bennett**
Publisher **The Boston Globe**
Category **Single Page/Spread**
Date **November 23, 1986**

285
Publication **New York University Magazine**
Art Director **Steven Hoffman**
Designer **Steven Hoffman**
Illustrator **Jamie Bennett**
Publisher **New York University**
Category **Single Page/Spread**
Date **Spring 1986**

286
Publication **The Boston Globe**
Art Director **Lynn Staley**
Designer **Gail Anderson**
Illustrator **Janet Knott**
Publisher **The Boston Globe**
Category **Single Page/Spread**
Date **December 7, 1986**

287

287A   287B   287C   287D

157

287
Publication **Life**
Art Director **Bob Ciano**
Designer **Nora Sheehan**
Illustrator **James McMullan**
Publisher **Time, Inc.**
Category **Story Presentation**
Date **June 1986**

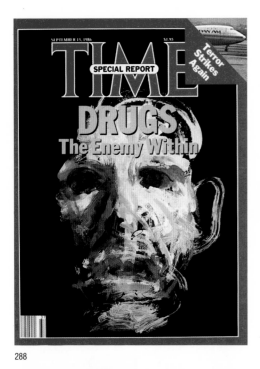

288

290

292

289

291

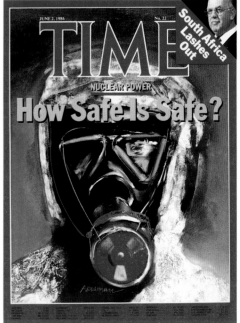

293

288
Publication **Time**
Art Director **Rudy Hoglund**
Illustrator **Allen Hirsch**
Publisher **Time, Inc.**
Category **Cover**
Date **September 15, 1986**

290
Publication **Time**
Art Director **Rudy Hoglund**
Illustrator **Robert Rauschenberg**
Publisher **Time, Inc.**
Category **Cover**
Date **January 6, 1986**

292
Publication **Time**
Art Director **Rudy Hoglund**
Illustrator **Seymour Chwast**
Publisher **Time, Inc.**
Category **Cover**
Date **April 14, 1986**

289
Publication **Time**
Art Director **Rudy Hoglund**
Illustrator **Allen Hirsch**
Publisher **Time, Inc.**
Category **Cover**
Date **April 21, 1986**

291
Publication **Time**
Art Director **Rudy Hoglund**
Illustrator **Roger Huyssen**
Publisher **Time, Inc.**
Category **Cover**
Date **November 10, 1986**

293
Publication **Time**
Art Director **Rudy Hoglund**
Illustrator **Marshall Arisman**
Publisher **Time, Inc.**
Category **Cover**
Date **June 2, 1986**

294

295

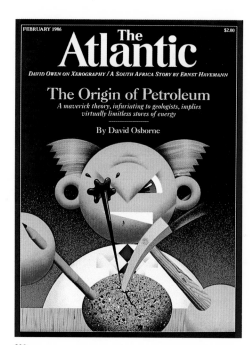

296

294
Publication **Time**
Art Director **Rudy Hoglund**
Illustrator **Gottfried Helnwien**
Publisher **Time, Inc.**
Category **Cover**
Date **October 6, 1986**

295
Publication **Time**
Art Director **Rudy Hoglund**
Illustrator **Guy Billout**
Publisher **Time, Inc.**
Category **Cover**
Date **March 24, 1986**

296
Publication **The Atlantic Monthly**
Art Director **Judy Garlan**
Designer **Judy Garlan**
Illustrator **Jose Cruz**
Publisher **The Atlantic Monthly Co.**
Category **Cover**
Date **February 1986**

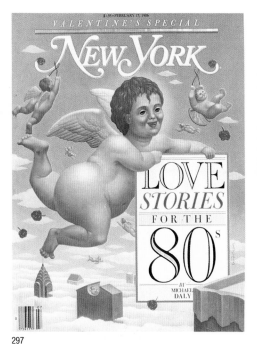

297

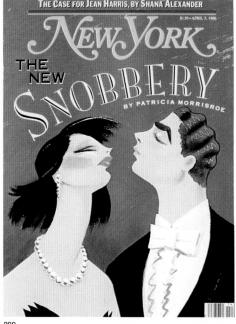

299

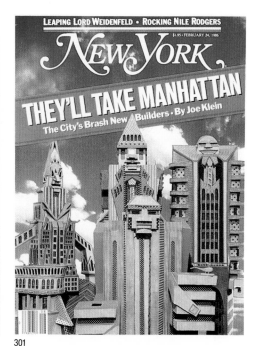

301

160

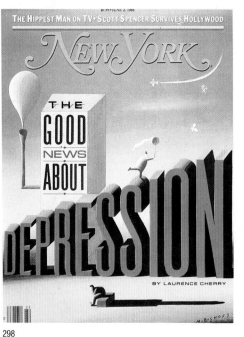

298

300

302

297
Publication **New York**
Art Director **Robert Best**
Designer **Josh Gosfield**
Illustrator **Robert Goldstrom**
Publisher **Murdoch Magazines, Inc.**
Category **Cover**
Date **February 17, 1986**

298
Publication **New York**
Art Director **Robert Best**
Designer **Josh Gosfield**
Illustrator **Maris Bishofs**
Publisher **Murdoch Magazines, Inc.**
Category **Cover**
Date **June 2, 1986**

299
Publication **New York**
Art Director **Robert Best**
Designer **Josh Gosfield**
Illustrator **Gary Hallgren**
Publisher **Murdoch Magazines, Inc.**
Category **Cover**
Date **April 7, 1986**

300
Publication **New York**
Art Director **Robert Best**
Designer **Josh Gosfield**
Publisher **Murdoch Magazines, Inc.**
Category **Cover**
Date **1986**

301
Publication **New York**
Art Director **Robert Best**
Designer **Josh Gosfield**
Publisher **Murdoch Magazines, Inc.**
Category **Cover**
Date **1986**

302
Publication **New York**
Art Director **Robert Best**
Designer **Josh Gosfield**
Publisher **Murdoch Magazines, Inc.**
Category **Cover**
Date **March 31, 1986**

303

304

303
Publication **Washington Post Magazine**
Art Director **Brian Noyes**
Designer **Brian Noyes**
Illustrator **Brad Holland**
Publisher **The Washington Post**
Category **Cover**
Date **November 30, 1986**

304
Publication **Washington Post Magazine**
Art Director **Brian Noyes**
Designer **Jann Alexander**
Illustrator **Carl Wesley**
Publisher **The Washington Post**
Category **Cover**
Date **October 26, 1986**

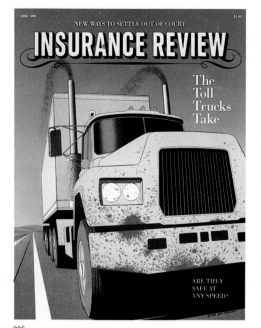

305

306

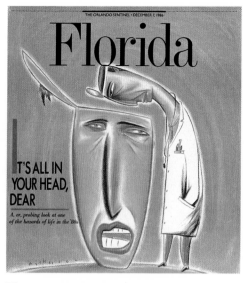

308

307

306
Publication **Enterprise**
Art Director **John Howze**
Designer **John Howze**
Illustrator **Rob Grace**
Publisher **Southwestern Bell Corp.**
Category **Cover**
Date **June 1986**

305
Publication **Insurance Review**
Art Director **Walter Bernard, Milton Glaser**
Designer **Colleen McCudden**
Illustrator **Guy Billout**
Publisher **Insurance Review**
Category **Cover**
Date **June 1986**

307
Publication **The Family Therapy Networker**
Art Director **Bevi Chagnon**
Designer **Bevi Chagnon, Marla Tarbox**
Illustrator **Marla Tarbox**
Publisher **The Family Therapy Network**
Category **Cover**
Date **November 1986**

308
Publication **Florida Magazine**
Art Director **Santa Choplin**
Designer **Santa Choplin**
Illustrator **Buddy Hickerson**
Publisher **Sentinel Communications Co.**
Category **Cover**
Date **December 7, 1986**

309

310

311

309
Publication **Drug Topics**
Art Director **Thomas Darnsteadt**
Designer **John Newcomb, Thomas Darnsteadt**
Illustrator **Brian Ajhar**
Publisher **Drug Topics**
Category **Cover**
Date **June 16, 1986**

310
Publication **The Plain Dealer Magazine**
Art Director **Gerard Sealy**
Designer **Gerard Sealy**
Illustrator **Merle Nacht**
Publisher **The Plain Dealer**
Category **Cover**
Date **December 14, 1986**

311
Publication **Phi Delta Kappan**
Illustrator **Brad Holland**
Category **Cover**
Publisher **Phi Delta Kappan**
Date **February 1986**

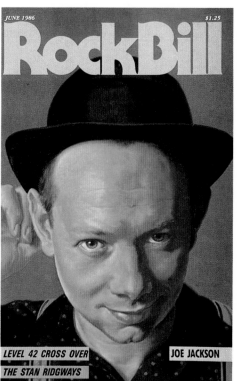

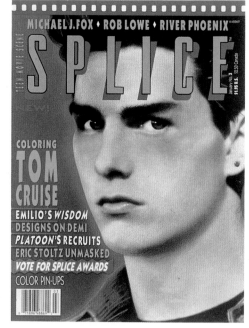

312

315

314

313
Publication **Rockbill**
Art Director **Cliff Sloan**
Designer **Cliff Sloan, Ken Joudrey**
Illustrator **Ken Joudrey**
Publisher **Rave Communications**
Category **Cover**
Date **June 1986**

312
Publication **Chicago**
Art Director **Robert J. Post**
Designer **Robert J. Post**
Illustrator **Brad Holland**
Publisher **WFMT, Inc.**
Category **Cover**
Date **August 1986**

314
Publication **Spy**
Art Director **Stephen Doyle**
Designer **Rosemarie Sohmer**
Photographer **Chris Callis**
Publisher **A/S/M Communications Co.**
Category **Cover**
Date **October 1986**

315
Publication **Splice**
Art Director **Robert Altemus**
Designer **Robert Altemus**
Illustrator **Susan Hall**
Photographer **Ron Phillips**
Publisher **Ira Friedman, Inc.**
Category **Cover**
Date **January 1986**

316

317

316
Publication **Florida Magazine**
Art Director **Santa Choplin**
Designer **Santa Choplin**
Illustrator **Gary Kelly**
Publisher **Sentinel Communications Co.**
Category **Cover**
Date **December 14, 1986**

317
Publication **Maxwell House Messenger**
Art Director **Janice Fudyma**
Designer **Janice Fudyma, Iris Brown**
Illustrator **Brian Ajhar**
Publisher **Maxwell House, General Foods Corp.**
Category **Cover**
Date **September 1986**

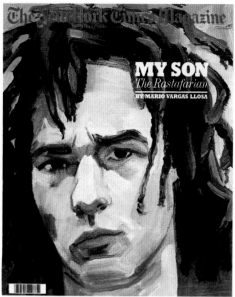

318

319

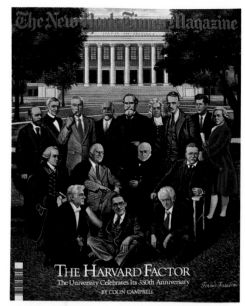

321

320

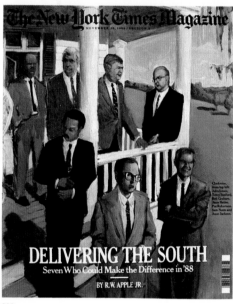

322

166

319
Publication **The New York Times Magazine**
Art Director **Ken Kendrick, Diana LaGuardia**
Designer **Ken Kendrick**
Illustrator **Guy Billout**
Publisher **The New York Times**
Category **Cover**
Date **June 8, 1986**

321
Publication **The New York Times Magazine**
Art Director **Ken Kendrick, Diana LaGuardia**
Designer **Kevin McPhee**
Illustrator **Teresa Fasolino**
Publisher **The New York Times**
Category **Cover**
Date **July 20, 1986**

318
Publication **The New York Times Magazine**
Art Director **Ken Kendrick, Diana LaGuardia**
Designer **Ken Kendrick**
Illustrator **Mike Glier**
Publisher **The New York Times**
Category **Cover**
Date **February 16, 1986**

320
Publication **The New York Times Magazine**
Art Director **Ken Kendrick, Diana LaGuardia**
Designer **Richard Samperi**
Illustrator **Peter De Seve**
Publisher **The New York Times**
Category **Cover**
Date **February 9, 1986**

322
Publication **The New York Times Magazine**
Art Director **Diana LaGuardia**
Designer **Diana LaGuardia**
Illustrator **Michael Paraskevas**
Publisher **The New York Times**
Category **Cover**
Date **November 30, 1986**

323

325

327

324

326

323
Publication **The New York Times**
Art Director **Nicki Kalish**
Designer **Nicki Kalish**
Illustrator **Ed Koren**
Publisher **The New York Times**
Category **Cover**
Date **January 1, 1986**

324
Publication **The New York Times**
Art Director **Nicki Kalish**
Designer **Nicki Kalish**
Illustrator **Laurent de Brunhoff**
Publisher **The New York Times**
Category **Cover**
Date **December 15, 1986**

325
Publication **The New York Times**
Art Director **Nicki Kalish**
Designer **Nicki Kalish**
Illustrator **Edward Gorey**
Publisher **The New York Times**
Category **Cover**
Date **June 4, 1986**

326
Publication **The New York Times**
Art Director **Nancy Sterngold**
Designer **Nancy Sterngold**
Illustrator **David Johnson**
Publisher **The New York Times**
Category **Cover**
Date **June 15, 1986**

327
Publication **The New York Times**
Art Director **Nicki Kalish**
Designer **Nicki Kalish**
Illustrator **Elwood Smith**
Publisher **The New York Times**
Category **Cover**
Date **August 27, 1986**

328

RECORDS

ELVIS COSTELLO'S CROWN OF THORNS

KING OF AMERICA
Elvis Costello ■ Columbia

BY MARK COLEMAN

330

RECORDS

Fogerty eyes the apocalypse

BY ANTHONY DeCURTIS

EYE OF THE ZOMBIE
John Fogerty ■ Warner Bros.

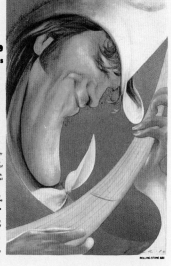

332

RECORDS

Tina repeats a winning formula

BY DAVITT SIGERSON

BREAK EVERY RULE
Tina Turner ■ Capitol

329

RECORDS

Cyndi's new shades

BY JIMMY GUTERMAN

TRUE COLORS
Cyndi Lauper ■ Portrait

331

RECORDS

He's got the big world in his hands

BIG WORLD
Joe Jackson ■ A&M

Joe Jackson's always been a little restless, and that's probably what's kept him around longer than most of the other late-Seventies nouveau punks. After emerging with a couple of Sixties-inspired power-pop albums in 1979, he shifted unhesitatingly into reggae, Forties swing, Latin-tinged urban pop and heavily orchestrated jazz. By the time he embraced George Gershwin and Cole

333

RECORDS

PETER GABRIEL: SO FAR, 'SO' GOOD

BY TIM HOLMES

SO
Peter Gabriel ■ Geffen

When Peter Ga-
b r i e l an-
nounced his depar-
ture from Genesis in
1975, a two-part
prognosis seemed
reasonable. Without
the flamboyant an-
tics of its frontman
— who might per-
form dressed as a
gigantic sunflower
one night and a pyr-
amid-headed psy-
chedelic druid the
next — Genesis
would founder, while

328
Publication **Rolling Stone**
Art Director **Derek Ungless**
Designer **Raul Martinez**
Illustrator **Ian Pollock**
Publisher **Straight Arrow Publishers**
Category **Single Page/Spread**
Date **March 27, 1986**

329
Publication **Rolling Stone**
Art Director **Derek Ungless**
Designer **Angelo Savaides**
Illustrator **Jose Cruz**
Publisher **Straight Arrow Publishers**
Category **Single Page/Spread**
Date **December 1986**

330
Publication **Rolling Stone**
Art Director **Derek Ungless**
Designer **Raul Martinez**
Illustrator **Steve Brodner**
Publisher **Straight Arrow Publishers**
Category **Single Page/Spread**
Date **November 20, 1986**

331
Publication **Rolling Stone**
Art Director **Derek Ungless**
Designer **Raul Martinez**
Illustrator **Michel Guire Vaka**
Publisher **Straight Arrow Publishers**
Category **Single Page/Spread**
Date **June 5, 1986**

332
Publication **Rolling Stone**
Art Director **Derek Ungless**
Designer **Raul Martinez**
Illustrator **Blair Drawson**
Publisher **Straight Arrow Publishers**
Category **Single Page/Spread**
Date **November 6, 1986**

333
Publication **Rolling Stone**
Art Director **Derek Ungless**
Designer **Raul Martinez**
Illustrator **Paola Piglia**
Publisher **Straight Arrow Publishers**
Category **Single Page/Spread**
Date **August 14, 1986**

334

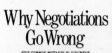

335

337

169

334
Publication **Rolling Stone**
Art Director **Derek Ungless**
Designer **Raul Martinez**
Illustrator **Phillip Burke**
Publisher **Straight Arrow Publishers**
Category **Single Page/Spread**
Date **October 9, 1986**

336
Publication **Science Digest**
Art Director **Michael Valenti**
Designer **David Bayer**
Illustrator **Marshall Arisman**
Publisher **The Hearst Corporation**
Category **Single Page/Spread**
Date **February 1986**

335
Publication **Psychology Today**
Art Director **Lester Goodman**
Designer **Anne DuVivier, Ann Stephens**
Illustrator **Cary Henrie**
Publisher **American Psychological Association**
Category **Single Page/Spread**
Date **June 1986**

337
Publication **Stereo Review**
Art Director **Sue Llewellyn**
Designer **Sue Llewellyn**
Illustrator **Lane Smith**
Publisher **CBS Magazines**
Category **Single Page/Spread**
Date **December 1986**

338

340

339

341

338
Publication **Playboy**
Art Director **Tom Staebler**
Designer **Kerig Pope**
Illustrator **Mel Odom**
Publisher **Playboy Enterprises, Inc.**
Category **Single Page/Spread**
Date **January 1986**

339
Publication **Playboy**
Art Director **Tom Staebler**
Designer **Kerig Pope**
Illustrator **Dave Calver**
Publisher **Playboy Enterprises, Inc.**
Category **Single Page/Spread**
Date **February 1986**

340
Publication **Playboy**
Art Director **Tom Staebler**
Designer **Theo Kouvatsos**
Illustrator **Robert Risko**
Publisher **Playboy Enterprises, Inc.**
Category **Single Page/Spread**
Date **June 1986**

341
Publication **Playboy**
Art Director **Tom Staebler**
Designer **Len Willis**
Illustrator **Don Baum**
Publisher **Playboy Enterprises, Inc.**
Category **Single Page/Spread**
Date **December 1986**

342

343

344

345

171

346

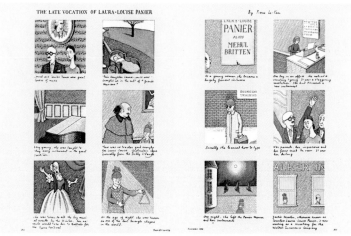

348

172

347

349

346
Publication **New Age Journal**
Art Director **Greg Paul**
Designer **Greg Paul**
Illustrator **Brad Holland**
Publisher **Rising Star Associates**
Category **Single Page/Spread**
Date **February 1986**

347
Publication **Manhattan, Inc.**
Art Director **Nancy Butkus**
Designer **Gina Davis**
Illustrator **Philippe Weisbecker**
Publisher **Metrocorp**
Category **Single Page/Spread**
Date **April 1986**

348
Publication **Town & Country**
Art Director **Melissa Tardiff**
Designer **Maria Cirillo**
Illustrator **John Glashan**
Publisher **The Hearst Corporation**
Category **Single Page/Spread**
Date **September 1986**

349
Publication **Town & Country**
Art Director **Melissa Tardiff**
Designer **Maria Cirillo**
Illustrator **Pierre LeTan**
Publisher **The Hearst Corporation**
Category **Single Page/Spread**
Date **November 1986**

350

352

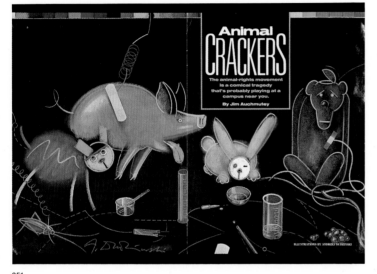

351

350
Publication **Campus Voice**
Art Director **Michael B. Marum**
Designer **Michael B. Marum**
Illustrator **Guy Billout**
Publisher **Whittle Communications**
Category **Single Page/Spread**
Date **April/May 1986**

351
Publication **Campus Voice**
Art Director **Su Pogany**
Designer **Su Pogany**
Illustrator **Andrez Dudzinski**
Publisher **Whittle Communications**
Category **Single Page/Spread**
Date **Winter 1986**

352
Publication **New York**
Art Director **Robert Best**
Designer **Josh Gosfield**
Illustrator **Vivienne Flesher**
Publisher **Murdoch Magazines, Inc.**
Category **Single Page/Spread**
Date **November 24, 1986**

THE GARDEN OF EDEN
by Ernest Hemingway

Illustrations by James McMullan

353

Most people thought they were brother and sister

Twice more the fish forced his way out

She looked at him with the laughing eyes

Why do we have to go by everyone else's rules?

353A   353B   353C   353D

174

353
Publication **Life**
Art Director **Bob Ciano**
Illustrator **James McMullan**
Publisher **Time, Inc.**
Category **Single Page/Spread**
Date **June 1986**

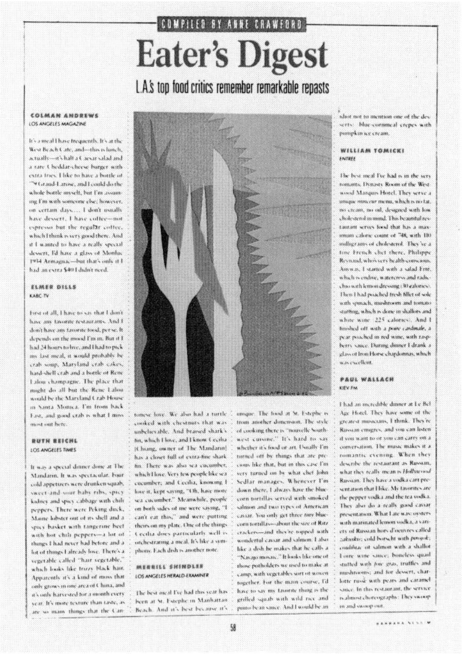
COMPILED BY ANNE CRAWFORD

Eater's Digest

L.A.'s top food critics remember remarkable repasts

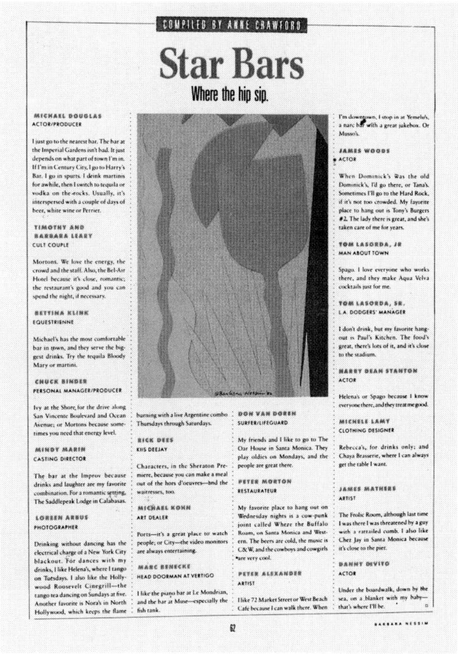
COMPILED BY ANNE CRAWFORD

Star Bars

Where the hip sip.

354

354A

354
Publication **L.A. Style**
Art Director **Rip Georges**
Designer **Rip Georges**
Illustrator **Barbara Nessim**
Publisher **L.A. Style, Inc.**
Category **Story Presentation**
Date **August 1986**

355

356

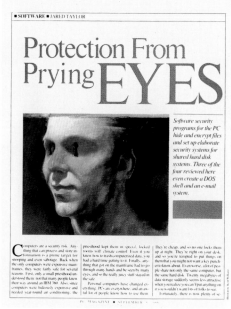

357

176

355
Publication **New York**
Art Director **Robert Best**
Designer **Josh Gosfield, Betsy Welsh**
Illustrator **David Suter**
Photo Editor **Susan Vermazen**
Publisher **Murdoch Magazines, Inc.**
Category **Single Page/Spread**
Date **October 1986**

356
Publication **Town & Country**
Art Director **Melissa Tardiff**
Designer **Richard Turtletaub**
Illustrator **Robert Goldstrom**
Publisher **The Hearst Corporation**
Category **Single Page/Spread**
Date **July 1986**

357
Publication **PC Magazine**
Art Director **Mary Zisk**
Designer **Esther Draznin**
Illustrator **Kent Williams**
Publisher **Ziff/Davis, Inc.**
Category **Single Page/Spread**
Date **September 16, 1986**

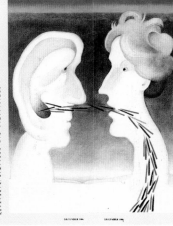

358

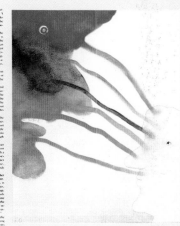

358A

358B

358
Publication **The Atlantic Monthly**
Art Director **Judy Garlan**
Designer **Judy Garlan**
Illustrator **Etienne Delessert**
Publisher **The Atlantic Monthly Co.**
Category **Story Presentation**
Date **November/December 1986**

Controversies in resuscitation

Daniel G. Hankins, MD

Preview
Many techniques and drugs for resuscitation are controversial. Do the risks of the esophageal obturator airway outweigh the advantages? Does the new cardiopulmonary resuscitation (CPR), with its techniques to change intrathoracic and intrabdominal pressures, represent an improvement over standard CPR? Does use of the antishock garment in CPR increase survival rates? Dr Hankins makes some interesting observations on these resuscitation techniques and discusses pharmacologic intervention with calcium, calcium channel blockers, and naloxone in cardiac arrest situations.

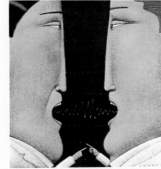

359

Pharmacotherapy for chronic obstructive pulmonary disease

Thomas L. Petty, MD

Preview
A family history of chronic airflow obstruction and a history of smoking along with evidence of airflow limitation are the most important indicators of the course of chronic obstructive pulmonary disease. In this article, Dr Petty outlines a pharmacologic strategy to improve and extend the lives of patients with all degrees of chronic obstructive pulmonary disease. He recommends a combination of smoking cessation, influenza virus vaccination, and pneumococcal vaccination once in a lifetime as the most effective measures to inhibit deterioration in ventilatory function. The systematic use of antimicrobials to ease exacerbations and the use of inhaled and oral bronchodilators to reverse airflow obstruction and corticosteroids to manage acute respiratory failure are effective in the majority of patients.

178

360

Sexuality in coronary artery disease
A problem-oriented approach

Francis G. Mackey, MD

Preview
The subject of sexuality is too often avoided or given short shrift by physicians dealing with patients who have had a myocardial infarction or coronary bypass surgery. These patients, seeking to return to a full and normal life-style, understandably ask themselves and their physicians questions about whether and when they can resume sexual activity and whether this can cause heart pain and/or further injury. As Dr Mackey points out, the large majority of cardiac patients can, indeed, be reassured that their sex life can continue normally, although several important problem areas need to be considered as part of a comprehensive rehabilitation program.

361

Lumbar disk disease
Clinical presentation, diagnosis, and treatment

Robert P. Durning, MD   Maureen L. Murphy, PA-C

Preview
Back pain seems almost ubiquitous in our society. Every day, physicians hear complaints of backaches, yet diagnosis is often difficult because of the need to rely on the patient's subjective interpretation of the pain. The most difficult clinical decisions arise when the history and physical examination are compelling and seem diagnostic of disk disease yet corroborative tests fail to demonstrate evidence of disease. In this exhaustive review, the authors discuss the clinical findings necessary for accurate diagnosis and treatment of lumbar disk disease.

362

359
Publication **Postgraduate Medicine**
Art Director **Tina Adamek**
Illustrator **Tom Curry**
Publisher **McGraw-Hill Publications**
Category **Single Page/Spread**
Date **May 15, 1986**

360
Publication **Postgraduate Medicine**
Art Director **Tina Adamek**
Illustrator **Matt Mahurin**
Publisher **McGraw-Hill Publications**
Category **Single Page/Spread**
Date **August 1986**

361
Publication **Postgraduate Medicine**
Art Director **Tina Adamek**
Illustrator **Mel Odom**
Publisher **McGraw-Hill Publications**
Category **Single Page/Spread**
Date **July 1986**

362
Publication **Postgraduate Medicine**
Art Director **Tina Adamek**
Illustrator **Enid Hatton**
Publisher **McGraw-Hill Publications**
Category **Single Page/Spread**
Date **April 1986**

363
Publication **Postgraduate Medicine**
Art Director **Tina Adamek**
Illustrator **John Jude Palencar**
Publisher **McGraw-Hill Publications**
Category **Single Page/Spread**
Date **October 1986**

364
Publication **Postgraduate Medicine**
Art Director **Tina Adamek**
Illustrator **David Frampton**
Publisher **McGraw-Hill Publications**
Category **Single Page/Spread**
Date **January 1986**

365
Publication **The Physician and Sportsmedicine**
Art Director **Tina Adamek**
Illustrator **Dale Gottlieb**
Publisher **McGraw-Hill Publications**
Category **Single Page/Spread**
Date **July 1986**

180

366

368

367

369

366
Publication **Emergency Medicine**
Art Director **Lois Erlacher**
Designer **Marlene Goldman**
Illustrator **Peter De Seve**
Publisher **McGraw-Hill Publications Co.**
Category **Single Page/Spread**
Date **October 15, 1986**

367
Publication **Emergency Medicine**
Art Director **Lois Erlacher**
Designer **Lois Erlacher**
Illustrator **Peter De Seve**
Publisher **McGraw-Hill Publications Co.**
Category **Single Page/Spread**
Date **February 1986**

368
Publication **Fine Dining**
Art Director **Georgina Sculco**
Designer **Georgina Sculco**
Illustrator **Carter Gooddrich**
Publisher **Cahners Publishing Co.**
Category **Single Page/Spread**
Date **December 1986**

369
Publication **Electronics Merchandising**
Art Director **Marjorie Crane**
Designer **Marjorie Crane**
Illustrator **Peter De Seve**
Publisher **CES Publishing, Inc.**
Category **Single Page/Spread**
Date **September 1986**

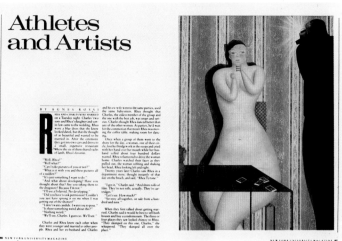

370

371

372

373

181

370
Publication **Building Profit**
Art Director **William Hillenbrand**
Designer **William Hillenbrand**
Illustrator **David K. Sheldon**
Publisher **Butler Manufacturing Co.**
Category **Single Page/Spread**
Date **Summer 1986**

371
Publication **Consumer Electronics**
Art Director **David Amario**
Designer **David Amario**
Illustrator **Andrew Shachat**
Publisher **International Thomson Retail Press**
Category **Single Page/Spread**
Date **February 1986**

372
Publication **New York University Magazine**
Art Director **Steven Hoffman**
Designer **Steven Hoffman**
Illustrator **Blair Dawson**
Publisher **New York University**
Category **Single Page/Spread**
Date **Winter 1986**

373
Publication **New York University Magazine**
Art Director **Steven Hoffman**
Designer **Steven Hoffman**
Illustrator **Alexa Grace**
Publisher **New York University**
Category **Single Page/Spread**
Date **Winter 1986**

374

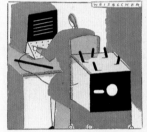

376

375
Publication **Byte Magazine**
Art Director **Nancy S. Rice**
Illustrator **Andrej Dudzinski**
Publisher **McGraw-Hill Publications**
Category **Single Page/Spread**
Date **September 1986**

374
Publication **Building Profit**
Art Director **William Hillenbrand**
Designer **William Hillenbrand**
Illustrator **David K. Sheldon**
Publisher **Butler Manufacturing Co.**
Agency **Wolf Blumberg Krody, Inc.**
Category **Single Page/Spread**
Date **Summer 1986**

376
Publication **Byte Magazine**
Art Director **Jan Muller**
Illustrator **Philippe Weisbecker**
Publisher **McGraw-Hill Publications Co.**
Category **Single Page/Spread**
Date **September 1986**

The Company Director: Executive On a Hotseat

377

TEEN SCENE

Are teens a prime target
for video? Some say yes.
☐ *By Mark Thalenberg*

379

Smart power: A smart way to regulate current in the 80s

A new $90 million market of semiconductors is
coming on stream for home-appliances

Home appliances will be the first big market for smart power chips

378

DOES WEIGHT LOSS SIGNIFY AN EATING DISORDER?

Emaciation may suggest anorexia nervosa, but it's also
necessary to explore the patient's feelings about
food and beliefs about her body. Thus, the history
is of paramount importance.

By Philip Kaminstein, MD

183

380

377
Publication **Industrial Launderer**
Art Director **Jack Lefkowitz**
Designer **Jack Lefkowitz**
Illustrator **Timothy Flatt**
Publisher **American Institute of
Industrial Launderers**
Category **Single Page/Spread**
Date **February 1986**

378
Publication **Electronic Business**
Art Director **William Cooke**
Designer **William Cooke**
Illustrator **Dave Joly**
Publisher **CES Publishing**
Category **Single Page/Spread**
Date **October 15, 1986**

379
Publication **Video Business**
Art Director **Mary Connolly**
Illustrator **Andrew Shachat**
Publisher **ITBP/Video Business**
Category **Single Page/Spread**
Date **November 1986**

380
Publication **Diagnosis**
Art Director **Carol Waters**
Designer **John Newcomb, Carol Walters**
Illustrator **Francis Jetter**
Publisher **Diagnosis Magazine**
Category **Single Page/Spread**
Date **November 1986**

381

DEPRESSION AT AN EARLY AGE

It strikes in childhood, and it's on the rise.

BY JOSEPH ALPER

When depression starts in childhood or adolescence, it is likely to have a genetic link.

381A

Between 1960 and 198 , the suicide rate among 15- to 19-year-olds increased by 136 percent.

381B

381
Publication **Science 86**
Art Director **John Isley**
Designer **John Isley**
Illustrator **Greg Spalenka**
Publisher **American Association for the Advancement of Science**
Category **Story Presentation**
Date **May 1986**

184

What really happened to Flight 007

"THE TARGET IS DESTROYED"

BY SEYMOUR M. HERSH

In Moscow

TODAY, THREE YEARS AFTER THE SOVIETS SHOT down Korean Air Lines Flight 007, killing all 269 people aboard, they remain convinced that some evidence somewhere will prove to the world that the airliner was sent over their skies by the Reagan Administration. In May of 1984, shortly after beginning research on Flight 007, I was granted permission to visit the Soviet Union and conduct interviews about it. My visit to Moscow culminated in a long meeting with Marshal Nikolai V. Ogarkov, the head of the Soviet General Staff, which oversees all Soviet military forces, and Deputy Foreign Minister Georgi M. Kornienko, in an ornate conference room belonging to the Defense Ministry. After five days of interviews and briefings, I had been provided with no evidence to support the thesis—which Ogarkov and Kornienko seemed to believe—that Flight 007 was a deliberate provocation. I raised what seemed to be the obvious questions. Why not simply tell the world. "We made a mistake and shot down the airliner in the belief that it was an American reconnaissance plane"? Why say that it had to be a spy plane when there obviously was no proof?

Kornienko answered by telling me why I had been invited to Moscow: he and Ogarkov had agreed to my visit in the hope that they could persuade me, as a journalist, to investigate the General Intelligence Agency's role in the shootdown. Taken aback, but realizing that the two senior Soviet officials were serious, I asked Kornienko with a laugh whether he was trying to be my editor. His response came in English: "Your assignment is to find that it was an attitude." The Deputy Foreign Minister added that the

This article is drawn from Mr. Hersh's book of the same name, which will be published this month by Random House.

47

382A

'I'LL BE THE DADDY...'

THE FACT THAT THE BOY BOUGHT HIS MOTHER A WARM COAT was not the disturbing part. The disturbing part, says Annette Mars Kastaloff of the Children's Group After School Program at Greenwich, 3.1—, is that the boy was thirteen.

"He saw it as a rummage sale and said, 'My mother doesn't have a warm coat.' I know that if like that. 'So he paid the $2 or whatever it cost. That's not appropriate for a child that age."

Or, to put it another way, 8-year-olds should not be thinking about whether their mothers needs a warm coat. It should be the other way around. Which means that in a real sense this boy is no longer a child. He is a short adult, a parent in disguise, a person who is already taking care of someone else instead of being taken care of himself.

Little kids who take care of their parents grow up with an insatiable need to be children.

BY ELLEN RITTBERG

ILLUSTRATION BY DAVE SHANNON

185

383

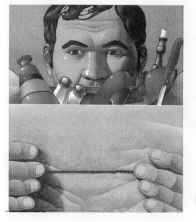

PARAPHERNALIA

BY KAREN LOEB

385

EXTREME UNCTION

BY BARNEY McCLELLAND

386

Publication **Audio Times**
Art Director **Daniel McDonald**
Designer **Daniel McDonald**
Illustrator **Joshua Schreier**
Publisher **International Thompson Retail Press**
Category **Single Page/Spread**
Date **June 1986**

Publication **Florida Magazine**
Art Director **Santa Choplin**
Designer **Santa Choplin**
Illustrator **Ray Mel Cornelius**
Publisher **Sentinel Communications Co.**
Category **Single Page/Spread**
Date **November 9, 1986**

Publication **Florida Magazine**
Art Director **Santa Choplin**
Designer **Santa Choplin**
Illustrator **Scott Mack**
Publisher **Sentinel Communications Co.**
Category **Single Page/Spread**
Date **December 14, 1986**

IS THE MIDDLE CLASS DOOMED?

By Barbara Ehrenreich

The author contends that the extremes of wealth and poverty are growing, moving America toward a two-tier society.

About Men

BY ERROLL MCDONALD

MYSTERY MAN

COOK, CHAUFFEUR, CRITIC—THE WHOLE IDEA WAS TO BECOME INDISPENSABLE

CONFESSIONS OF A STEPMOTHER

By Dalia Epstein

A MASTER'S MIND

AN UNPUBLISHED STORY
SHEDS NEW LIGHT ON HENRY JAMES'S
ART AND SEXUALITY

By Cynthia Ozick

HUGH MERROW

By Henry James

387
Publication **The New York Times Magazine**
Art Director **Diana LaGuardia**
Designer **Kevin McPhee**
Illustrator **Randall Enos**
Publisher **The New York Times**
Category **Single Page/Spread**
Date **September 7, 1986**

388
Publication **The New York Times Magazine**
Art Director **Diana LaGuardia**
Designer **Audry Razgaitis**
Illustrator **Paola Piglia**
Publisher **The New York Times**
Category **Single Page/Spread**
Date **December 14, 1986**

388
Publication **The New York Times Magazine**
Art Director **Diana LaGuardia**
Designer **Audrey Razgaitis**
Illustrator **Paola Piglia**
Publisher **The New York Times**
Category **Single Page/Spread**
Date **December 14, 1986**

390
Publication **The New York Times Magazine**
Art Director **Diana LaGuardia**
Designer **Audrey Razgaitis**
Illustrator **Paola Piglia**
Publisher **The New York Times**
Category **Single Page/Spread**
Date **December 14, 1986**

393

394

391

188

392

391
Publication **The Scientist**
Art Director **Wayne Fitzpatrick**
Designer **Wayne Fitzpatrick**
Illustrator **Anthony Russo**
Publisher **Eugene Garfield/I.S.I.**
Category **Single Page/Spread**
Date **November 17, 1986**

392
Publication **The Scientist**
Art Director **Wayne Fitzpatrick**
Designer **Wayne Fitzpatrick**
Illustrator **David Shannon**
Publisher **Eugene Garfield/I.S.I.**
Category **Single Page/Spread**
Date **December 15, 1986**

393
Publication **Spy**
Art Director **Stephen Doyle**
Designer **Rosemarie Sohmer**
Illustrator **Bill Russell**
Publisher **A/S/M Publications Co.**
Category **Story Presentation**
Date **November 1986**

394
Publication **National Geographic**
Art Director **Howard E. Paine**
Illustrator **Karel Havlicek**
Publisher **The National Geographic Society**
Category **Single Page/Spread**
Date **February 1986**

BOATS REMEMBERED

395

395A

395
Publication **Nautical Quarterly**
Art Director **Clare Cunningham**
Designer **Clare Cunningham**
Illustrator **Jeffrey Smith**
Publisher **Nautical Quarterly**
Category **Story Presentation**
Date **June 1986**

396

396
Publication **The New York Times**
Art Director **Jerelle Kraus**
Designer **Jerelle Kraus**
Illustrator **Rafael Olbinski**
Publisher **The New York Times**
Category **Single Page/Spread**
Date **November 6, 1986**

ERASING THE PAST

Europe's Amnesia About the Holocaust

MORE THAN 40 YEARS have passed since the end of World War II. Yet despite a wide-spread desire to suppress the nightmarish memories of the war and the Holocaust...

By Judith Miller

Bitburg in Germany, Waldheim in Austria, Barbie in France—new societies rest on buried, but very uneasy, memories.

Candles, 113 of them, once flared in Brooklyn to honor the dead in a Jewish family, shot on the Russian border.

PERHAPS NO COUNTRY WAS EXPLORED in recent past as intensively as the Federal Republic of Germany...

Scratch the surface and distinct recollections of the war erupt, with astonishing bitterness and hatred.

WHEN BURT WALLACE THE WALDHEIM...

397
Publication **The New York Times Magazine**
Art Director **Diana LaGuardia**
Designer **Audrey Razgaitis**
Illustrator **Matt Mahurin, Sheldon Greenburg,
Paola Piglia**
Publisher **The New York Times**
Category **Story Presentation**
Date **November 16, 1986**

397A

397B

398

398A

398B

398
Publication **The New York Times Magazine**
Art Director **Diana LaGuardia**
Designer **Diana LaGuardia**
Photographer **Michael O'Neill**
Publisher **The New York Times**
Category **Story Presentation**
Date **March 23, 1986**

A NEW GENERATION OF JUDGES AND OFFICIALS has declared all-out war on the Mafia in Sicily. The battle is being waged in the courts, in the political arena and in the streets of Palermo, Sicily's principal city. Two photographers, Letizia Battaglia from Palermo and Franco Zecchin, a Milanese, in the course of working for a Sicilian daily newspaper, L'Ora, joined the campaign, seeking to inform and educate the public about the Mafia. For the last six years, they have been documenting the violence and corruption synonymous with the Mafia and recording the arduous struggle to make justice, at long last, prevail on the island.

SICILY MAFIA

Photographs by Letizia Battaglia and Franco Zecchin

399

For years, the Mafia seemed to act with impunity. Empowered by new, tougher laws, and using informers willing to break the traditional code of silence, Italian prosecutors are on the offensive, risking their lives to save their countrymen's.

399A

Fighting the Mafia, according to political leaders, means bringing Sicily out of the poverty and isolation that have long been its lot. Sicily is changing, and its attitude toward the Mafia is changing along with it, but the process is a slow one.

399B

399
Publication **The New York Times Magazine**
Art Director **Ken Kendrick, Diana LaGuardia**
Designer **Ken Kendrick**
Photographer **Letizia Battaglia, Franco Zecchin**
Publisher **The New York Times**
Category **Story Presentation**
Date **May 18, 1986**

400

400A

194

400B

400
Publication **The New York Times Magazine**
Art Director **Ken Kendrick, Diana LaGuardia**
Designer **Ken Kendrick**
Photographer **Peter Lindbergh**
Publisher **The New York Times**
Category **Story Presentation**
Date **May 18, 1986**

401

401A

401B

401
Publication **Bride's Magazine**
Art Director **Phyllis Richmond Cox**
Designer **Phyllis Richmond Cox**
Photographer **Sheila Metzner**
Publisher **Conde Nast Publications, Inc.**
Category **Story Presentation**
Date **December 1986**

LADIES IN WAITING

402

THE ROLLING STONE INTERVIEW
JACK NICHOLSON

BY FRED SCHRUERS

Jack Nicholson's Hollywood Hills home perches above an empty ravine – a rare prospect amid these overbuilt hills of dirt and scrub. On the hot afternoon when I arrive, a chain-link fence is being installed (not, I'm later told, at Nicholson's instigation) on the winding driveway he shares with Marlon Brando. Despite the fence and an electronic inspection of visitors, Nicholson's complex – two houses, a row of carports topped by a basketball hoop, and a deck equipped with a pool and a commanding

403

TIP O'NEILL'S LAST HURRAH

Tip O'Neill could not have planned a more graceful exit. The elections last month gave his beloved Democratic party a majority in both houses of the Congress. His own seat in the House of Representatives, which he is relinquishing after thirty-four years, passed with his blessing to Joseph P. Kennedy II – the nephew of John F. Kennedy, whom O'Neill succeeded in the seat in 1953. Only five years after the lowest point of his career – when he was openly ridiculed by the Republicans, the press and some members of his own party – the Speaker of the House came down from the Hill to tell the American people, "The Reagan revolution is over."

The rise of Thomas P. O'Neill is a story of the old politics. His grandfather came from County Cork, Ireland, to settle in North Cambridge, Massachusetts, where he found work as a bricklayer. His father started a small contracting business there and was elected to the city council. O'Neill entered the Massachusetts state legislature at the age of twenty-four – and has held public office ever since.

In 1952, JFK ran for the U.S. Senate; a year earlier he had privately

BY WILLIAM GREIDER
PHOTOGRAPH BY NIGEL DICKSON

404

402
Publication **Rolling Stone**
Art Director **Derek Ungless**
Designer **Angelo Savaides**
Photographer **Matthew Rolston**
Publisher **Straight Arrow Publishers**
Category **Single Page/Spread**
Date **April 24, 1986**

403
Publication **Rolling Stone**
Art Director **Derek Ungless**
Designer **Raul Martinez**
Photographer **Herb Ritts**
Publisher **Straight Arrow Publishers**
Category **Single Page/Spread**
Date **August 14, 1986**

404
Publication **Rolling Stone**
Art Director **Derek Ungless**
Designer **Raul Martinez, Angelo Savaides**
Photographer **Nigel Dickson**
Publisher **Straight Arrow Publishers**
Category **Single Page/Spread**
Date **December 18, 1986**

405

405A

405B

405
Publication **Rolling Stone**
Art Director **Derek Ungless**
Designer **Derek Ungless**
Photographer **Michael O'Brien**
Publisher **Straight Arrow Publishers**
Category **Story Presentation**
Date **November 20, 1986**

198

Permanent
WAVE

*Sebou the Imperial
turns the heads of New York's
crème de la crème*

BY JOYCE WADLER

406A

*Sebou can
do a cut in three
minutes. As
quickly, David
Brown says, as a
barber in the army*

406B

*This business
hasn't made us
wealthy," says
Richard, "it's
made us well-
known"*

406C

*Richard
often wakes
sleeping clients
with a kiss. "The
Cinderella
Thing," he calls it*

406
Publication **Manhattan, Inc.**
Art Director **Nancy Butkus**
Designer **Nancy Butkus**
Photographer **Larry Fink**
Publisher **Metrocorp**
Category **Story Presentation**
Date **September 1986**

The Serengeti
A Portfolio
By MITSUAKI IWAGO

407

Shimmering abstractions, zebras may seek safety by joining a   river of wildebeests migrating across the plains in spring.

407A

407B

407

Publication **National Geographic**
Art Director **Gerard A. Valerio**
Designer **Gerard A. Valerio**
Photo Editor **Rob Hernandez**
Photographer **Mitsuaki Iwago**
Publisher **The National Geographic Society**
Category **Story Presentation**
Date **May 1986**

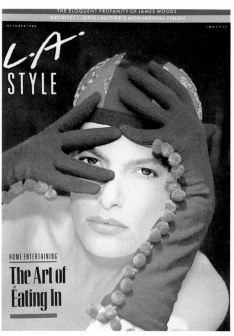

408

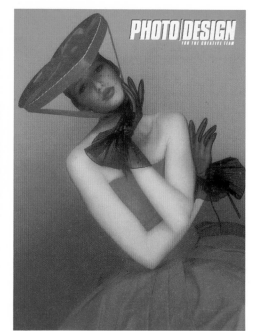

410

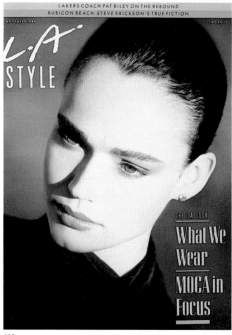

409

411

408
Publication **L.A. Style**
Art Director **Rip Georges**
Designer **Rip Georges**
Photographer **Phillip Dixon**
Publisher **L.A. Style, Inc.**
Category **Cover**
Date **October 1986**

409
Publication **L.A. Style**
Art Director **Rip Georges**
Designer **Rip Georges**
Photographer **Phillip Dixon**
Publisher **L.A. Style, Inc.**
Category **Cover**
Date **November 1986**

410
Publication **Photo/Design**
Art Director **Deborah Lewis**
Photographer **Richie Williamson**
Publisher **Lakewood Publications**
Category **Cover**
Date **March/April 1986**

411
Publication **Photo/Design**
Art Director **Deborah Lewis**
Photographer **Irvin Blitz**
Publisher **Lakewood Publications**
Category **Cover**
Date **September/October 1986**

412

414

413

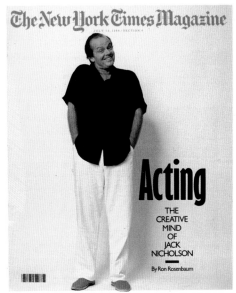

415

412
Publication **Manhattan, inc.**
Art Director **Nancy Butkus**
Designer **Nancy Butkus**
Photographer **George Large**
Publisher **Metrocorp**
Category **Cover**
Date **October 1986**

413
Publication **Manhattan, inc.**
Art Director **Nancy Butkus**
Designer **Nancy Butkus**
Photographer **William Coupon**
Publisher **Metrocorp**
Category **Cover**
Date **June 1986**

414
Publication **The New York Times Magazine**
Art Director **Diana LaGuardia**
Designer **Diana LaGuardia**
Photographer **Michael O'Neill**
Publisher **The New York Times**
Category **Story Presentation**
Date **March 23, 1986**

415
Publication **The New York Times Magazine**
Art Director **Diana LaGuardia**
Designer **Diana LaGuardia**
Photographer **Michael O'Neill**
Publisher **The New York Times**
Category **Cover**
Date **July 13, 1986**

416

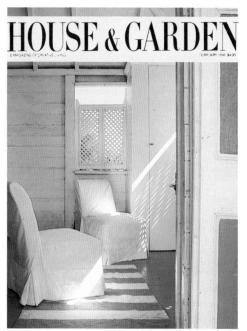

417

416
Publication **Progressive Architecture**
Art Director **Richelle J. Huff**
Designer **Richelle J. Huff**
Photographer **Luis Casals**
Publisher **Penton Publishing Co.**
Category **Cover**
Date **June 1986**

417
Publication **House & Garden**
Art Director **Lloyd Ziff, Karen Lee Grant**
Designer **Lloyd Ziff**
Photographer **Francois Halard**
Publisher **Conde Nast Publications, Inc.**
Category **Cover**
Date **February 1986**

418

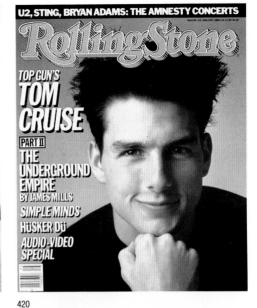

420

419

421

418
Publication **Rolling Stone**
Art Director **Derek Ungless**
Designer **Derek Ungless**
Photographer **Matthew Rolston**
Publisher **Straight Arrow Publishers**
Category **Cover**
Date **October 9, 1986**

420
Publication **Rolling Stone**
Art Director **Derek Ungless**
Designer **Derek Ungless**
Photographer **Herb Ritts**
Publisher **Straight Arrow Publishers**
Category **Cover**
Date **June 19, 1986**

419
Publication **Rolling Stone**
Art Director **Derek Ungless**
Designer **Derek Ungless**
Photographer **Bonnie Shiffman**
Publisher **Straight Arrow Publishers**
Category **Cover**
Date **March 27, 1986**

421
Publication **Rolling Stone**
Art Director **Derek Ungless**
Designer **Derek Ungless**
Photographer **Matthew Rolston**
Publisher **Straight Arrow Publishers**
Category **Cover**
Date **June 5, 1986**

Rodney Dangerfield has wealth, fame, a hit movie and the respect of almost everybody but himself. Life, whew, it's rough. By Lewis Grossberger

RESPECT AT LAST

Hot Rodney!

So now it's Rodney the movie star. Five years ago, last time I talked to him, he was merely America's fastest-rising old comedian. Now he's Rodney, summer-film comet. Every time you turn around, the guy's career goes up a notch.

We're in the back of a chauffeured stretch with all the trimmings. Bar, TV, phone are all ignored. Rodney is spooning up a big bowl of cereal, fruit and skim milk. He's on some kind of diet kick, making a stab at health, not too optimistically. "I got no willpower, forget it, will ya? It's

422

THE RETURN OF THE INVISIBLE MAN

What is William Burroughs, the father of the Beat Generation and author of 'Naked Lunch,' doing in Lawrence, Kansas? Trying to shoot his way from time into space.

By James Fox

WILLIAM BURROUGHS PHOTOGRAPHED IN LAWRENCE, KANSAS, BY NIGEL DICKSON

424

BY FRED SCHRUERS

PHOTOGRAPH BY MATTHEW ROLSTON

CAN'T STOP THE GIRL

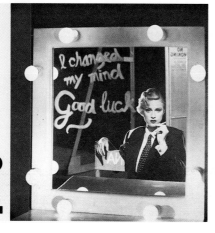

204 423

Tom Cruise made the teen flick Risky Business. Now the ace is wild in Top Gun.

WINGING IT

BY CHRISTOPHER CONNELLY

425

422
Publication **Rolling Stone**
Art Director **Derek Ungless**
Designer **Raul Martinez**
Photographer **Deborah Feingold**
Publisher **Straight Arrow Publishers**
Category **Single Page/Spread**
Date **August 28, 1986**

423
Publication **Rolling Stone**
Art Director **Derek Ungless**
Designer **Raul Martinez**
Photographer **Matthew Rolston**
Publisher **Straight Arrow Publishers**
Category **Single Page/Spread**
Date **June 5, 1986**

424
Publication **Rolling Stone**
Art Director **Derek Ungless**
Designer **Angelo Savaides**
Photographer **Nigel Dickson**
Publisher **Straight Arrow Publishers**
Category **Single Page/Spread**
Date **October 23, 1986**

425
Publication **Rolling Stone**
Art Director **Derek Ungless**
Designer **Derek Ungless**
Photographer **Herb Ritts**
Publisher **Straight Arrow Publishers**
Category **Single Page/Spread**
Date **June 19, 1986**

A Night in the Bushes

Far from the Mattingly crowd, a minor-league game offers the true baseball believer some major pleasures

By Richard Ford

THE ROLLING STONE INTERVIEW
BILLY JOEL

The atmosphere at Kaufman Astoria Studios in Queens combines all the giddiness and physical discomfort of a back-to-school shopping spree. Billy Joel has interrupted rehearsals for his first tour in nearly three years to sample the latest fashions for potential stage wear – and he's getting expert advice from his wife, model Christie Brinkley, who is sitting on the floor with their nine-month-old daughter, Alexa Ray.

BY ANTHONY DeCURTIS PHOTOGRAPH BY ALBERT WATSON

426

427

426
Publication **Rolling Stone**
Art Director **Derek Ungless**
Designer **Derek Ungless**
Photographer **Michael Geiger**
Publisher **Straight Arrow Publishers**
Category **Single Page/Spread**
Date **1986**

427
Publication **Rolling Stone**
Art Director **Derek Ungless**
Designer **Raul Martinez**
Photographer **Albert Watson**
Publisher **Straight Arrow Publishers**
Category **Single Page/Spread**
Date **November 6, 1986**

205

428

429

430

206

431

428
Publication **Psychology Today**
Art Director **Lester Goodman**
Designer **Anne DuVivier, Ann Stephens**
Photographer **Ed Kashi**
Publisher **American Psychological Association**
Category **Single Page/Spread**
Date **January 1986**

429
Publication **American Photographer**
Art Director **Howard Klein**
Designer **Howard Klein**
Photographer **Elizabeth Zeschin**
Publisher **CBS, Inc.**
Category **Single Page/Spread**
Date **November 1986**

430
Publication **Manhattan, Inc.**
Art Director **Nancy Butkus**
Designer **Nancy Butkus**
Photographer **Jonathan Becker**
Publisher **Metrocorp**
Category **Single Page/Spread**
Date **June 1986**

431
Publication **Success**
Art Director **David Bayer**
Designer **David Bayer**
Photographer **Britain Hill**
Photo Editor **Pat Cadley**
Publisher **Hal Publications**
Category **Single Page/Spread**
Date **November 1986**

432

433

432
Publication **House & Garden**
Art Director **Lloyd Ziff, Karen Lee Grant**
Designer **Karen Lee Grant**
Photographer **Marina Slhinz**
Publisher **Conde Nast Publications, Inc.**
Category **Single Page/Spread**
Date **December 1986**

433
Publication **House & Garden**
Art Director **Lloyd Ziff, Karen Lee Grant**
Designer **Lloyd Ziff**
Photographer **Timothy Hursley**
Publisher **Conde Nast Publications, Inc.**
Category **Single Page/Spread**
Date **July 1986**

208

434
Publication **Us Magazine**
Art Director **Robert Priest**
Designer **Janet Waegel**
Photographer **E.J. Camp**
Publisher **Us Magazine Co.**
Category **Single Page/Spread**
Date **January 13, 1986**

435
Publication **Us Magazine**
Art Director **Robert Priest**
Designer **Janet Waegel**
Photographer **Lara Rossignol**
Publisher **Us Magazine Co.**
Category **Single Page/Spread**
Date **February 10, 1986**

436
Publication **Us Magazine**
Art Director **Robert Priest**
Designer **Janet Waegel**
Photographer **Mark Hanauer**
Publisher **Us Magazine Co.**
Category **Single Page/Spread**
Date **July 14, 1986**

437
Publication **Us Magazine**
Art Director **Robert Priest**
Designer **Janet Waegel**
Photographer **Larry Williams**
Publisher **Us Magazine Co.**
Category **Single Page/Spread**
Date **April 21, 1986**

438
Publication **Us Magazine**
Art Director **Robert Priest**
Designer **Robert Priest**
Photographer **Briam Smale**
Publisher **Us Magazine Co.**
Category **Single Page/Spread**
Date **August 11, 1986**

439
Publication **Spy**
Art Director **Stephen Doyle**
Designer **Rosemarie Sohmer**
Photographer **George Hein**
Publisher **A/S/M Publications Co.**
Category **Single Page/Spread**
Date **October 1986**

Pictures of the Year

440

The most elegant, entrancing, exacting—and English—of all desserts.

Crème Brûlée

By James Villas

441

A Lesson In Tragedy

By C. D. B. Bryan

Seven years ago, astronaut Ellison Onizuka wrote to a boy—about space, technology and fun. Last month, Derek went to watch Challenger fly

442

CLASSIC PORTRAIT

W-154

The perfect 1930s racer of smooth, two-part extravagance: a vintage-racing car connoisseur and a master mechanic.

by William Jeanes

443

440
Publication **Sports Illustrated**
Art Director **Steven Hoffman**
Designer **Steven Hoffman**
Photographer **Chuck Solomon**
Publisher **Time, Inc.**
Category **Single Page/Spread**
Date **December 22, 1986**

441
Publication **Town & Country**
Art Director **Melissa Tardiff**
Designer **Melissa Tardiff**
Photographer **Julian Calder**
Publisher **The Hearst Corporation**
Category **Single Page/Spread**
Date **April 1986**

442
Publication **The New York Times Magazine**
Art Director **Diana LaGuardia**
Designer **Diana LaGuardia**
Photographer **Jeanne Strongin**
Publisher **The New York Times**
Category **Single Page/Spread**
Date **February 23, 1986**

443
Publication **Mercedes Magazine**
Art Director **John Tom Cohoe**
Designer **John Tom Cohoe**
Photographer **Brad Miller**
Agency **McCaffrey McCall**
Category **Single Page/Spread**
Date **Spring 1986**

FINDING A LOST WORLD

A newly discovered record of a proud Southern society that few people ever thought existed

In 1920, when Richard Samuel Roberts's name first appeared in the Columbia, South Carolina, city directory—in the "Colored Dept."—he was listed as a janitor in the post office. He continued in that job, the kind of job a black was expected to have in his strictly segregated city, even after he had established an ambitious photography business in the black community. Self-taught, he learned his craft by studying brochures and catalogs sent by supply houses. The result was an extraordinary array of dignified and beautiful pictures of a little-known society. Now, fifty years after his death, Roberts's photographs have been rediscovered. The glass negatives, which were stored in the crawl space under the family house, have been retrieved and many of the subjects painstakingly identified. A book of these photographs, *A True Likeness: The Black South of Richard Samuel Roberts, 1920–1936,* edited by Thomas L. Johnson and Phillip C. Dunn, will be published this fall by Bruccoli Clark/Algonquin Books of Chapel Hill.—B.K.

During a delivery to Williams' Drug Store on Gervais Street, the unidentified driver of a Julep Line soft-drink truck poses with his vehicle. Note the 1920s-style solid rubber tires.

88   AMERICAN HERITAGE

444

The flowers and table used as props in the studio shot opposite add to the freshness and delicacy Roberts emphasized in this portrait of an unidentified young woman (1920s).

Dressed up in hair ribbon and Mary Janes, this fierce girl does not seem pleased at having her picture taken. She is sitting defiantly on her toes in a apparently rocker on a front porch.

444A

444B

211

444
Publication **American Heritage**
Art Director **Beth Whitaker**
Designer **Beth Whitaker**
Photographer **Richard Samuel Roberts**
Publisher **Heritage Publications/Forbes**
Category **Story Presentation**
Date **October/November 1986**

445

ARTISTRY

446

212

445A

446A

446B

445
Publication **Bride's Magazine**
Art Director **Phyllis Richmond Cox**
Designer **Betty Berman Saronson**
Photographer **Bruce Wolf**
Publisher **Conde Nast Publications, Inc.**
Category **Story Presentation**
Date **June 1986**

446
Publication **Bride's Magazine**
Art Director **Phyllis Richmond Cox**
Designer **Ann Marie Amarino**
Photographer **James Wojcik**
Publisher **Conde Nast Publications, Inc.**
Category **Story Presentation**
Date **August 1986**

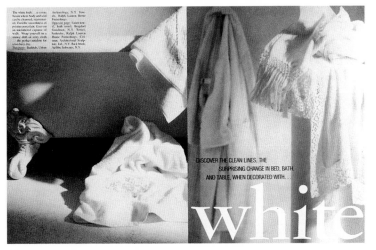

447

447A

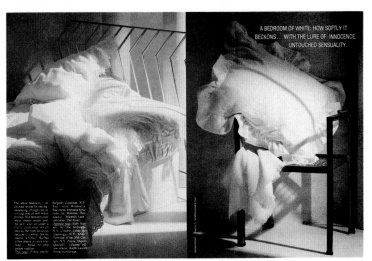

447B

447
Publication **Bride's Magazine**
Art Director **Phyllis Richmond Cox**
Designer **Betty Berman Saronson**
Photographer **Vanni Burkhart**
Publisher **Conde Nast Publications, Inc.**
Category **Story Presentation**
Date **October 1986**

GLITTERY GOLD TOUCHES

Shimmering gold accents spell excitement—when paired with bridal ivory and white. Gilded shoes add glamour to the new ankle-skimming hems jewelry, aglow with gemstones, smolders against folds of silk. This page: Ivory silk charmeuse gown with open V-back. Pearl draping at hips, wrists, bias-cut skirt melting into chapel train. By Andrea for Bridal Couture, about $1,200. Earrings, Diane Bell for D&E. Gloves, Carolina Amato. Hair, Bruce Libre. Opposite page: Metallic gold and mauve pump (top), unwrapped, gold leather pump (center); gold-heeled Fortuny fabric pump (bottom), all by Vittorio Ricci, N.Y. Earring (top), Kenneth Jay Lane. Gold jewelry, Ben Amun.

448

GRACEFUL NIGHT MOVES

A dancer's movement influence lingerie now. Ballerina styles gently sculpt the body, present to myself or enjoy. Here, a cowl-neck slips to the V-back in silk charmeuse (left). A slip of lace pins the simple liquid satin slip (right). Blue satin envelops vision in a robe. Opposite: White silk charmeuse gown à harmony of satin and chiffon. By Lynell for, about $140. Hair, makeup, Toshiko. This page: White, crushed liquid satin gown, French Lyons lace at bodice in dropped waist, satin body blue. Day, about $175. Ring, The Galaxie Diamond. Hair, makeup, Pat Carroll.

449

SPARKLING ALLURE: SHIMMERING COLORS

Glistening pumps, shimmers, jewels add a whimsical bridal touch... a prism of polish to color-sparked gowns. This page: Charmeuse gown in pink metallic. Full bow with trailing streamers cascading from bias-draped collar to floor. Beaded appliqués swirling on bodice. A chapel train. By Zuri for Joelle, about $1,200. Ribbon, Offray. Opposite page: Handset rhinestone pump (top), Imps. White sequin pump (center), Imps. Rhinestone-heeled satin shoe (bottom), Dynabbe. Brooch, rhinestone cuff, Pelwin. Multi-colored dangle earrings, Kenneth Jay Lane. Colored crystal bracelets, earring (bottom), Haison Designes for D&E. Hair, Bruce Libre. Lush, floral scent. Decadence by Parfums International.

448A

214

GRACEFUL NIGHT MOVES

Matching ensembles are the news in slip—and soft. Feather Wear, the ultimate gown in silk charmeuse robe blurs what's bed in favorable. Sumptuous as so for the slotless satin, slippery drama in one dimensional setting new dimensions in "featur" image. A chiffon of the gown (right), one cardigan slip to an everyday glistening lavender. This page: Silk charmeuse with length gown (left), satin, de flowing, about $170. Slip for French, Lynell bias, makeup, Toshiko. Opposite page: White sensi gown, quilted jacket. By Dior silk gown, about $140. Hair, makeup, Toshiko. $175. Hair, makeup, Toshiko.

449A

GRACEFUL NIGHT MOVES

Lingerie now evokes many images. The right version of your wedding dress—alive with peach evergreen. Delicate detail that baby. It turned jacket reaches to the satin-soft water. The sheer tape—a seduction of his style, unmistakably in silk charmeuse for a pajama and robe delay. The top robe in a glamorous nightshirt. Opposite page: Ivory satin gown, quilted jacket. By Dior Nikonos Gown, about $85. Jacket, about $600. Hair, makeup, Toshiko. This page: Sheer silk charmeuse pajamas, white robe. By Calvin Klein Underwear and Sleepwear. Pajamas, about $71. Robe, about $195. Hair, makeup, Pat Carroll.

449B

448
Publication **Bride's Magazine**
Art Director **Phyllis Richmond Cox**
Designer **Phyllis Richmond Cox**
Photographer **Eric Boman**
Publisher **Conde Nast Publications, Inc.**
Category **Story Presentation**
Date **June 1986**

449
Publication **Bride's Magazine**
Art Director **Phyllis Richmond Cox**
Designer **Betty Berman Saronson**
Photographer **Vanni Burkhart**
Publisher **Conde Nast Publications, Inc.**
Category **Story Presentation**
Date **October 1986**

450

450A

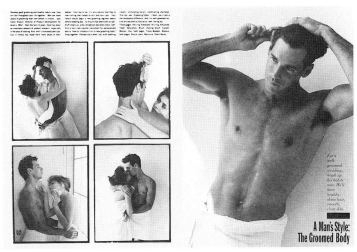

450B

450
Publication **Bride's Magazine**
Art Director **Phyllis Richmond Cox**
Designer **Betty Berman Saronson**
Photographer **Douglas Keeve**
Publisher **Conde Nast Publications, Inc.**
Category **Story Presentation**
Date **April 1986**

451

451B

451A

451C

451
Publication **Chicago Magazine**
Art Director **Robert J. Post**
Designer **Cynthia Hoffman**
Photographer **Victor Skrebneski**
Publisher **WFMT, Inc.**
Category **Story Presentation**
Date **September 1986**

Weekends Free
by Brenda Shapiro
wearing clothes for letting go

452

452A

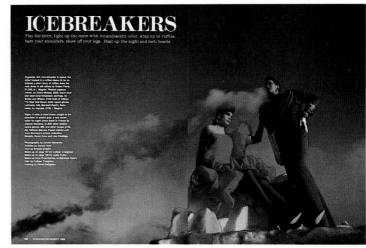

ICEBREAKERS
Play the siren, light up the room with incandescent color, wrap in ruffles, bare your shoulders, show off your legs. Heat up the night and melt hearts

453

217

452
Publication **Chicago Magazine**
Art Director **Robert J. Post**
Designer **Cynthia Hoffman**
Photographer **J. Verser Engelhard**
Publisher **WFMT, Inc.**
Category **Story Presentation**
Date **April 1986**

453
Publication **Chicago Magazine**
Art Director **Robert J. Post**
Designer **Cynthia Hoffman**
Photographer **Dennis Manarchy**
Publisher **WFMT, Inc.**
Category **Story Presentation**
Date **December 1986**

454

454A

454B

454
Publication **Town & Country**
Art Director **Melissa Tardiff**
Designer **Melissa Tardiff**
Photographer **Victor Skrebneski**
Publisher **The Hearst Corporation**
Category **Story Presentation**
Date **February 1986**

455

455A

455B

455
Publication **Town & Country**
Art Director **Melissa Tardiff**
Designer **Mary Rosen**
Photographer **Victor Skrebneski**
Publisher **The Hearst Corporation**
Category **Story Presentation**
Date **November 1986**

Washington's Living Monuments

By their parts shall ye know them

456

456A

220

456
Publication **Time**
Art Director **Tom Bentkowski**
Photographer **Eric Medla, Dennis Brack,
Black Star, Ted Thai, Neil Leiffer**
Publisher **Time, Inc.**
Category **Story Presentation**
Date **July 14, 1987**

At First Baptist of Georgetown, Tradition Reigns Beside God

457

457A

457
Publication **Washington Post Magazine**
Art Director **Jann Alexander**
Photographer **Maria Stenzel**
Publisher **The Washington Post**
Category **Story Presentation**
Date **December 21, 1986**

The NEW Wall Street

Long a warren of narrow, crooked streets and scrunched-up buildings, the world's greatest financial center is bursting out into a bigger, finer, more livable place. The lords of finance are expanding the district's battlements by building grand new headquarters on the banks of the Hudson and East rivers. Former commuters are homesteading in stylish new apartment complexes. And the cheerful renovation of the South Street Seaport wharf attracts a convivial young crowd that stays until well into the once desolate night.

Photographs by Jan Staller

Already hailed as the Next Great Place to live in the Big Apple, Battery Park City takes shape on a Hudson River landfill at the foot of the mammoth World Trade Center. Merrill Lynch and American Express are now headquartered in the two towers at left, part of the World Financial Center. Residential buildings in the middle and at right will contain some 14,000 luxury apartments. In the red-brick buildings, designed to evoke traditional Manhattan architecture, condos start at $181,000.

458

458A

Peeking out between the World Trade towers is the tip of the Woolworth Building, built for $13 million in 1913 and the world's tallest until 40 Wall Street topped it in 1929. Dow Jones and Oppenheimer are divvying up space in the copper-domed building in the middle and the granite tower at right—the south corner of the $1.5-billion World Financial Center. The white modular residential buildings at bottom and on the left predate the carefully controlled plans for the rest of the project.

458C

A Beaux Arts monument, the muraled U.S. Custom House at the southern end of Broadway is one of many historical buildings in the area that are being renovated. Limestone statues outside represent different continents; the murals inside depict ocean liners in New York City's harbor. Prospective tenants include the Museum of the American Indian and a federal bankruptcy court.

This cavernous glass pavilion between the American Express and Merrill Lynch towers will soon be turned into a winter garden, filled with 40-foot-high palm trees from the Mojave Desert (currently learning to live with less light under shade screens). Covering an area the size of Grand Central Station, the atrium will include luxury stores and be used for dance, theater, and art exhibitions.

Like a seagoing liner glimmering at night, another residential building goes up in Battery Park City. Once complete, this shell will be covered with white stone on the first two floors and brick above—two of the development's guidelines set down by architects Alexander Cooper and Stanton Eckstut. Another guideline: Building height must vary to echo Manhattan's jagged skyline.

458B

221

Scrubbed up Schermerhorn Row, a block of Georgian-Federal commercial buildings that line one side of the South Street Seaport plaza, houses a gaggle of trendy boutiques, restaurants, and bars. The plaza, located on the East River, has become an after-hours magnet for Wall Street's tired and weary. They don't have to come far. The new Prudential-Bache Securities Building, for instance, anchors one corner of the plaza. Says a bartender at the North Star Pub, where a draft of Watney's costs $4: "Wall Street used to be dark and deserted at night, but now the problem is getting them out of here."

458D

458
Publication **Fortune**
Art Director **Margery Peters**
Designer **Margery Peters, Holly Matteson**
Photographer **Jan Staller**
Publisher **Time, Inc.**
Category **Story Presentation**
Date **November 10, 1986**

MORE THAN SKIN DEEP

Architect Franklin D. Israel boldly restructures the
New York loft of make-up artist Francis R. Gillette

BY SUZANNE STEPHENS   PHOTOGRAPHS BY LANGDON CLAY

459

Two interior "houses," one with a red wall, the other marked by outside stairs leading to a sleeping alcove, occupy the center of the rooftop space. In the "courtyard" are a Duggie Fields painting, *Frayed Around the Edges*, and English Art Deco tub chairs.

459B

222

Francis Gillette (often called Rick) is known for the supreme sense of perfection he brings to hair and make-up in beauty and fashion photography. Lithe and trim of build, he would resemble the young Franchot Tone except that his own facial features usually remain immobile, setting off the intensity of his gaze. Short pauses separate his carefully chosen words. Right away you know this is a person with deeply felt convictions. "Part of the reason I came down to the financial district was to have a studio where I could take photos [another of his preoccupations] and entertain my friends, many of whom are artists and designers. But it was also an opportunity to create an environment with a very good friend—Frank Israel—who happens to be a leading architect," Gillette says. "But," he adds, "the apartment had to represent my point of view—my way of seeing and treating things."

Mood, color, changes of light, texture, and the tactile feeling of space here were all affected by that point of view: Gillette was so concerned about getting the blue stain of the concrete floor the exact shade that he mixed it and applied it himself—adding boxes of blue iridescent eye shadow (which he would rather not see on eyelids) to a dry pigment and alcohol base.

Some architects would toss in the T-square before allowing a

The main rooms are nestled in gabled alcoves arrayed around the perimeter of the rooftop studio, grouping pages. A freestanding fireplace, a painting by Francis Gillette's brother, Richard, Ivory Coast fabrics, and a one-armed plywood chair from the 1950s highlight the living area. *Above* An Art Deco desk of fruit and olive woods, which was designed for a yacht, is in he converted alabaster area. *Opposite* Windows of stippled and tinted glass, designed by the client, afford glimpses of rooftop ornament and the Manhattan skyline, including the Woolworth Building.

459A

A ceramic vase covered by glass shards set into a concrete coating, in the living area, opposite, was designed by Dan Bitter. Behind is a cast stone sculpture from the 1920s.

459C

At the entry, colored stucco finishes, a sliding wood grill gate leading into the first "house," and the grilled window of the house beyond evoke the vernacular architecture of warm climates.

459
Publication **House & Garden**
Art Director **Lloyd Ziff, Karen Lee Grant**
Designer **Lloyd Ziff**
Photographer **Langdon Clay**
Publisher **Conde Nast Publications, Inc.**
Category **Story Presentation**
Date **January 1986**

JOURNEY THROUGH SPACE

Christophe de Menil's search for a uniquely personal environment

BY JESSE KORNBLUTH
PHOTOGRAPHS
BY SHEILA METZNER

460

460B

460A

460C

223

460
Publication **House & Garden**
Art Director **Lloyd Ziff, Karen Lee Grant**
Designer **Lloyd Ziff**
Photographer **Sheila Metzner**
Publisher **Conde Nast Publications, Inc.**
Category **Story Presentation**
Date **February 1986**

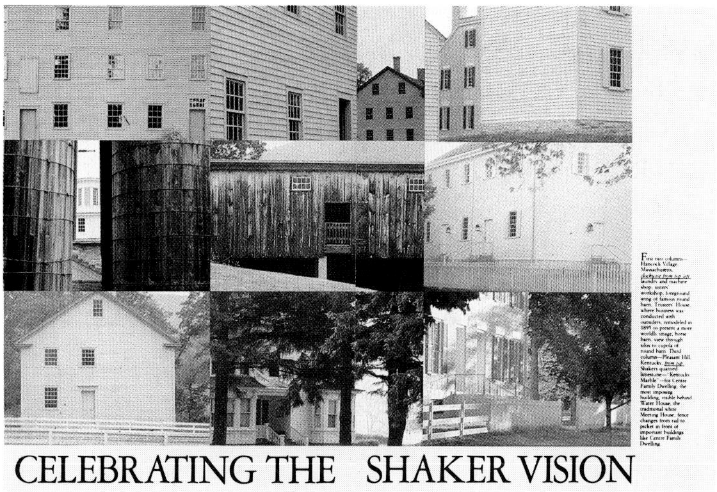
CELEBRATING THE SHAKER VISION
First two columns—Hancock Village, Massachusetts, clockwise from top left: laundry and machine shop, sisters' workshop, foreground wing of famous round barn, Trustees' House, where business was conducted with outsiders, remodeled in 1895 to present a more worldly image, horse barn, view through silos to cupola of round barn. Third column—Pleasant Hill, Kentucky, from top: Shakers quarried limestone—"Kentucky Marble"—for Centre Family Dwelling, the most imposing building, visible behind Water House, the traditional white Meeting House, fence changes from rail to picket in front of important buildings like Centre Family Dwelling.

461

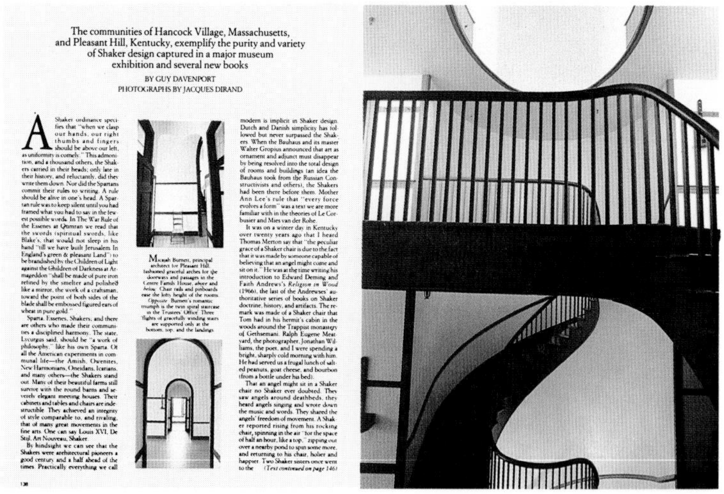

The communities of Hancock Village, Massachusetts, and Pleasant Hill, Kentucky, exemplify the purity and variety of Shaker design captured in a major museum exhibition and several new books

BY GUY DAVENPORT
PHOTOGRAPHS BY JACQUES DIRAND

A Shaker ordinance specifies that "when we clasp our hands, our right thumbs and fingers should be above our left, as uniformity is comely." This admonition, and a thousand others, the Shakers carried in their heads; only late in their history, and reluctantly, did they write them down. Nor did the Spartans commit their rules to writing. A rule should be alive in one's head. A Spartan rule was to keep silent until you had framed what you had to say in the fewest possible words. In The War Rule of the Essenes at Qumran we read that the swords (spiritual swords, like Blake's, that would not sleep in his hand "till we have built Jerusalem In England's green & pleasant Land") to be brandished by the Children of Light against the Children of Darkness at Armageddon "shall be made of pure iron refined by the smelter and polished like a mirror, the work of a craftsman, toward the point of both sides of the blade shall be embossed figured ears of wheat in pure gold."

Sparta, Essenes, Shakers; and there are others who made their communities a disciplined harmony. The state, Lycurgus said, should be "a work of philosophy," like his own Sparta. Of all the American experiments in communal life—the Amish, Owenites, New Harmonians, Oneidans, Icarians, and many others—the Shakers stand out. Many of their beautiful farms still survive with the round barns and severely elegant meeting houses. Their cabinets and tables and chairs are indestructible. They achieved an integrity of style comparable to, and rivaling, that of many great movements in the fine arts. One can say Louis XVI, De Stijl, Art Nouveau, Shaker.

By hindsight we can see that the Shakers were architectural pioneers a good century and a half ahead of the times. Practically everything we call modern is implicit in Shaker design. Dutch and Danish simplicity has followed but never surpassed the Shakers. When the Bauhaus and its master Walter Gropius announced that art as ornament and adjunct must disappear by being resolved into the total design of rooms and buildings (an idea the Bauhaus took from the Russian Constructivists and others), the Shakers had been there before them. Mother Ann Lee's rule that "every force evolves a form" was a text we are more familiar with in the theories of Le Corbusier and Mies van der Rohe.

It was on a winter day in Kentucky over twenty years ago that I heard Thomas Merton say that "the peculiar grace of a Shaker chair is due to the fact that it was made by someone capable of believing that an angel might come and sit on it." He was at the time writing his introduction to Edward Deming and Faith Andrews's *Religion in Wood* (1966), the last of the Andrewses' authoritative series of books on Shaker doctrine, history, and artifacts. The remark was made of a Shaker chair that Tom had in his hermit's cabin in the woods around the Trappist monastery of Gethsemani. Ralph Eugene Meatyard, the photographer, Jonathan Williams, the poet, and I were spending a bright, sharply cold morning with him. He had served us a frugal lunch of salted peanuts, goat cheese, and bourbon (from a bottle under his bed).

That an angel might sit in a Shaker chair no Shaker ever doubted. They saw angels around deathbeds, they heard angels singing and wrote down the music and words. They shared the angels' freedom of movement. A Shaker reported rising from his rocking chair, spinning in the air "for the space of half an hour, like a top," zipping out over a nearby pond to spin some more, and returning to his chair, holier and happier. Two Shaker sisters once went to the (Text continued on page 146)

Micajah Burnett, principal architect for Pleasant Hill, fashioned graceful arches for the doorways and passages in the Centre Family House, *above* and *below*. Chair rails and pinboards ease the lofty height of the rooms. *Opposite*: Burnett's romantic triumph is the twin spiral staircase in the Trustees' Office. Three flights of gracefully winding stairs are supported only at the bottom, top, and the landings.

138

461B

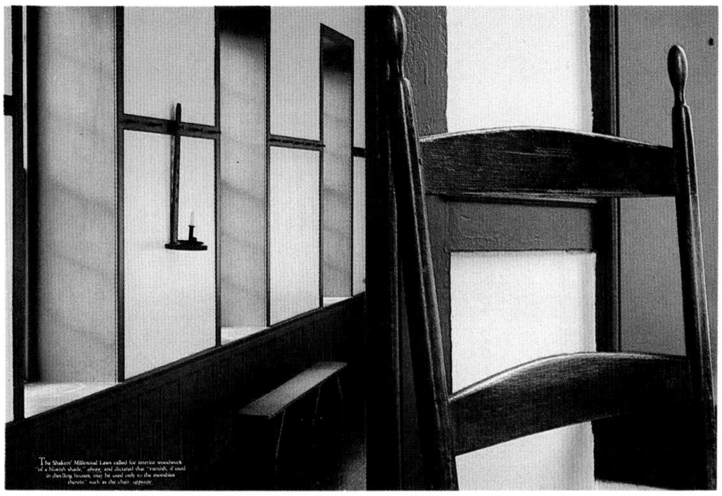
The Shakers' Millennial Laws called for interior woodwork "of a blueish shade," above, and dictated that "varnish, if used in dwelling houses, may be used only to the moveables therein" such as the chair, opposite.

461A

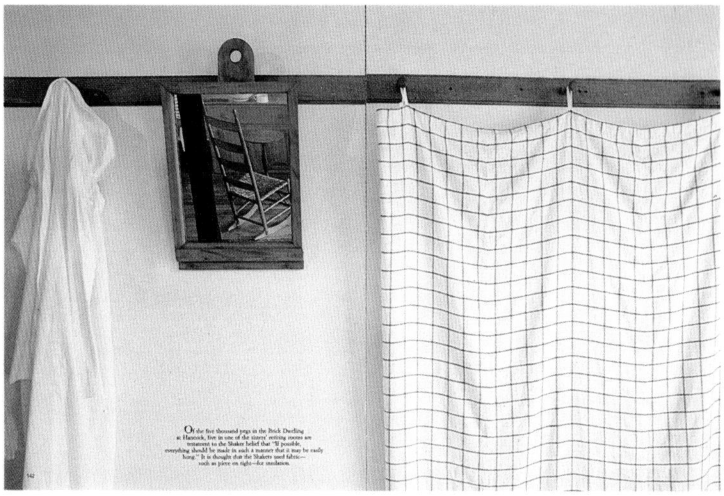
Of the five thousand pegs in the Brick Dwelling at Hancock, five in one of the sisters' retiring rooms are testament to the Shaker belief that "If possible, everything should be made in such a manner that it may be easily hung." It is thought that the Shakers used fabric—such as piece on right—for insulation.
142

461C

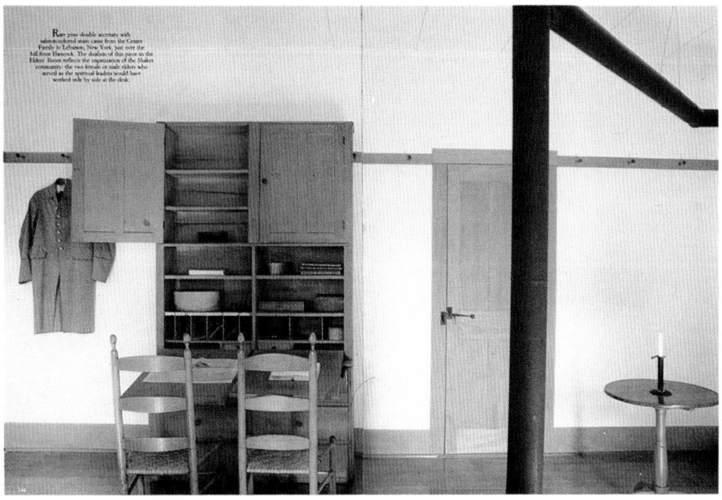
Rare pine double secretary with salmon-colored stain came from the Centre Family in Lebanon, New York, just over the hill from Hancock. The dualism of this piece in the Elders' Room reflects the organization of the Shaker community: the two female or male elders who served as the spiritual leaders would have worked side by side at the desk.

461D

461
Publication **House & Garden**
Art Director **Lloyd Ziff, Karen Lee Grant**
Designer **Karen Lee Grant**
Photographer **Jacques Dirand**
Publisher **Conde Nast Publications, Inc.**
Category **Story Presentation**
Date **July 1986**

This low, open meeting room was once filled for Shaker services at eight in the evening.

The United Society of Believers in Christ's Second Appearing worked hard for every one of its possessions, including its familiar name—the Shakers. Exhorted by an elder to "Shake off the flesh," arms, legs, heads, entire bodies obeyed. Believers sometimes shook for hours on end. Invaded by the spirit, they spoke in tongues, sensing the Devil's presence in a meetinghouse, the congregation rushed in circles, banishing evil with sweeping gestures of the hands. As the United Society spread beyond the original settlement near Albany, New York, its leaders imposed order on spiritual frenzy. Speaking in tongues became a repertory of carefully rehearsed song. The spontaneous twitching, swirling and lurching of individual worshipers gave way to communal dances so disciplined that an English traveler was reminded of military drills.

Devoted pacifists, the Shakers thought of themselves more as builders than as soldiers. Believing that an orderly existence here on earth earned one a place in heaven, the Shakers tried to give every detail of their lives a self-evident clarity. Our fascination with their crafts, and perhaps our yearning for a simpler lifestyle, have meant a resurgence in the collection and reproduction of all things Shaker. Though we can rarely see their communities at work, or these spiritual Utopias at worship, a current

The Shaker rocking chair is a classic.

462A

An elder's coat is suspended from yet another Shaker innovation—the coat hanger.

462B

Shaker crafts: the tinsmith shapes a bowl's rim.

The spinner begins another skein of wool.

A baker slices doughy cinnamon rolls.

Eldress Gertrude Soule, 92, of Canterbury.

462C

AMAZING GRACE

The artful simplicity of America's Shakers

BY CARTER RATCLIFF
PHOTOGRAPHED BY MICHAEL MELFORD

The spare, disciplined harmony of Shaker buildings is caught in early-morning sunlight at the Hancock Village in western Massachusetts.

462

462
Publication **Travel & Leisure**
Art Director **Adrian Taylor**
Designer **Adrian Taylor**
Photographer **Michael Melford**
Publisher **American Express Publishing Co.**
Category **Cover**
Date **September 1986**

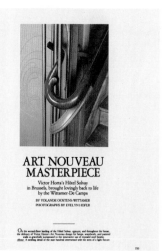

ART NOUVEAU
MASTERPIECE

Victor Horta's Hôtel Solvay
in Brussels, brought lovingly back to life
by the Wittamer-De Camps

BY YOLANDE OOSTENS-WITTAMER
PHOTOGRAPHS BY EVELYN HOFER

On the second-floor landing of the Hôtel Solvay, opposite, and throughout the house, the delicacy of Victor Horta's Art Nouveau design for lamps, woodwork, and painted walls is gracefully juxtaposed to the innovative use of exposed steel beams. *Above:* A swirling detail of the stair banded intertwined with the stem of a light fixture.

463

463B

226

463A

463C

463
Publication **House & Garden**
Art Director **Lloyd Ziff, Karen Lee Grant**
Photographer **Evelyn Hoper**
Publisher **Conde Nast Publications, Inc.**
Category **Story Presentation**
Date **October 1986**

Vienna 1900: To the Age, Its Art

From Klimt's golden paintings to Otto Wagner's architectural masterpieces, Vienna's
Jugendstil is being rediscovered by a generation eager to explore the apogee of Austrian culture.
By Wendy Lyon Moonan/Photographs by Derry Moore

"We can't change it inside or out; it's protect-
ed by the government," explains Dr.
Kurt Vignich, a political economist, above
with his wife Sonja in the grand entry
of the 1900 Villa Vignich. Dr. Vignich's great
uncle was doctor to Otto Wagner, then
Vienna's most revered architect, creator of
the city's gilded railway stations and

the monumental Church Am Steinhof. When
the doctor asked Wagner to build him
a house on the outskirts of town, Wagner
turned to his talented pupil Otto
Schönthal, who designed a mansion with
imaginative megalon ornamentation
on the outside (left) and organic motifs
in its white plaster on the walls within.

April, 1986   191

464

464A

464B

227

464
Publication **Town & Country**
Art Director **Melissa Tardiff**
Designer **Richard Turtletaub**
Photographer **Derry Moore**
Publisher **The Hearst Corporation**
Category **Story Presentation**
Date **April 1986**

**PHOTOGRAPHY BY
JOEL MEYEROWITZ**

Vision of Cape Cod

465

MINUS TIDES

466

466A

466B

465
Publication **Oceans Magazine**
Art Director **Adriane Stark**
Designer **Adriane Stark**
Photographer **Joel Meyerowitz**
Publisher **Oceans Magazine Associates**
Category **Story Presentation**
Date **January 1986**

466
Publication **Oceans Magazine**
Art Director **Adriane Stark**
Designer **Adriane Stark**
Photographer **David Schrader**
Publisher **Oceans Magazine Associates**
Category **Story Presentation**
Date **August 1986**

467

467A

467
Publication **House & Garden**
Art Director **Lloyd Ziff, Karen Lee Grant**
Designer **Marie-Paule Pelle**
Photographer **Francois Halard**
Publisher **Conde Nast Publications, Inc.**
Category **Story Presentation**
Date **August 1986**

COVER STORY

The Lady's Party

She had the biggest birthday ever, and why not?

For four golden days and gaudy nights, she was the still point of a turning, kaleidoscopic world. Immovable, she gazed upon the revelry with her forthright, rather stern expression. While not exactly a wallflower at her own birthday party, she appeared slightly aloof, distant. What's the big fuss? she might have been thinking. The question is understandable: after 100 years there is little the old girl has not seen before. But as an immigrant herself, she is perhaps even more sensitive to the curious ways of her adopted country, silently indulgent of good old American exuberance, excess and, yes, glitz. Though millions of visitors gawked at her, perhaps no one looked quite closely enough. Let them cavort, she seemed to say with an imperceptible smile. Liberty may be proud, but she isn't haughty. Look again. Was that—could it have been—a wink?

The Statue of Liberty is a sculpted symbol of freedom, an icon of democracy clothed in copper and iron. But the idea of Liberty Weekend for most people was simply to have fun, to watch ships passing under the sun and fireworks blossoming under the stars, to feel good about themselves because they felt good about their country, to feel proud of being proud.

As many as 6 million people descended upon the tip of Manhattan Island for the big show. Families from Wyoming and Kansas and Florida camped where yellow cabs usually scuffle; they picnicked where soulless stockbrokers, lawyers and city clerks scurry. New York was a time warp as thousands of white-suited sailors painted the town red. Ambling around Times Square, they transformed the city into a stage set from *On the Town* ("New York, New York, a helluva town/ The Bronx is up, but the Battery's down").

New York harbor was speckled with whitecaps and the wakes of some 20,000 boats of every conceivable shape and size. Their wild variety mirrored the diversity of the immigrants who passed through Ellis Island: Dutch flat-bottomed boats, Chinese junks, plush French yachts, Norwegian barkentines. Draped over one small vessel was a hand-lettered banner: OK. U.K. 1776 IS FORGIVEN. COME HOME COLONIALS. TEA AND CRUMPETS AWAIT.

The schools of small boats gave way to the majestic masters of the daylight

Let her be lit

hours, the 22 tall ships from 18 countries. The stately succession of tall ships was a graceful ambassador from a vanished, less hectic age. As a cool breeze billowed sails and spirits and Navy guns fired in salute, some spectators reacted with the quiet awe that is more commonly found in gazing at great cathedrals. "I feel like I'm watching history," said Julie Cook of Brookville, Pa. She was indeed.

Standing watch over the elegant sailing ships were the massive, muscular vessels of war: destroyers, frigates, the battleship *Iowa* and the aircraft carrier *John F. Kennedy*, from which the President and Mrs. Reagan surveyed the harbor and the Friday-night fireworks. Those leviathans provoked a different reaction, a buoyant chauvinism. As a crowded Staten Island ferryboat passed by the *Kennedy*, one sightseer called out, to cheers and laughter, "Come on over, Gaddafi!"

Liberty Weekend, some carped, was more about profits than patriotism, more about commerce than comity. The opening-night ceremony was a sentimentalized show-biz tribute that left no cliché unturned, a hokey combination of the old Jackie Gleason show from Miami Beach, the Rose Bowl parade and the Ziegfeld Follies. But what, after all, could be more American than that? Show biz, not solemnity, is an American hallmark; taste is not guaranteed in the Bill of Rights. President Reagan's aides were concerned that their

man would be demeaned by the Busby Berkeley choreography. Others joked about his pressing the game-show-size button to flash a laser beam that lighted the Lady. A malfunction, and there goes Star Wars. But the old actor, like the old gal to whom he paid tribute, seemed to rise above the script, as they say in Hollywood, and share the dignity that she never lost. His words were simple and heartfelt: "We are the keepers of the flame of liberty; we hold it high tonight for the world to see."

A televised naturalization ceremony that night for 16,000 immigrants in five cities was an exercise in satellite democracy. On Ellis Island, Chief Justice Warren Burger led the new Americans, live and remote, in reciting the Oath of Allegiance. Off-camera, Burger was followed by U.S. District Court Judge Mark A. Costantino, the son of parents from Rome and Naples, who exhorted the crowd with a more plain-spoken vision of citizenship: "Take a real good look at each other. What do you see? You see people of all races, all colors, all creeds. What do we do in America when we meet people? We shake hands. C'mon, shake hands! When you've shaken hands, you can say that you are real Americans."

In his speech that preceded Saturday's dazzling fireworks, President Reagan said 5½ years in the White House have left him with one overriding impression: "That the things that unite us—America's past of which we are so proud, our hopes and aspirations for the future of the world and this much loved country—these things far outweigh what little divides us."

Much still divides Americans, but Liberty Weekend united nearly everyone in a celebration of the statue and ourselves. "This country needs these things every ten years or so," said one spectator. Despite the gimcrackery, this was a people's holiday: the fireworks high above the harbor were the dazzling signature of a democratic free-for-all, overwhelming the staginess that came before and afterward. The Fourth of July weekend revealed, once again, the American spirit of freedom—and the freedom to be in high spirits, as the album of enduring images on the following pages will testify.
*—By Richard Stengel.
Reported by Bonnie Angelo and Cathy Booth/ New York*

10

468

230

468
Publication **Time**
Art Director **Tom Bentkowski**
Photographer **Eric Meola, Dennis Brack, Ted Thai,
Neil Leifer, Diana Walker**
Publisher **Time, Inc.**
Category **Story Presentation**
Date **July 14, 1986**

468A

468B

468C

469

231

469A

469B

469
Publication **Time**
Art Director **John White**
Photographer **Matt Mahurin**
Publisher **Time, Inc.**
Category **Story Presentation**
Date **March 17, 1986**

Family Album

What do you do when Mom and Dad are on the cutting edge of hip? Try a little one-upmanship? Go ultrapunk or ultraprep? Either way, you could end up looking like a rebel without a cause. Smart kids don't mind if the battle lines between the generations are blurred, as long as the styles are clearly in focus. Take a look at these celebrity offspring – proud to pose with their celebrity parents.

FASHION BY LAURIE SCHECHTER

CY CURNIN AND SON JAMIE

Photographs by RICHARD CORMAN

ROLLING STONE ISSUE 484

470

232

TOMMY CHONG AND DAUGHTER RAE DAWN

MICHELLE PHILLIPS AND DAUGHTER CHYNNA

470A

JIMMIE VAUGHAN AND DAUGHTER TINA

GEORGE CLINTON AND SON TRACEY

470B

JIMMY WEBB AND SONS

470C

470
Publication **Rolling Stone**
Art Director **Derek Ungless**
Designer **Derek Ungless**
Photographer **Richard Corman**
Publisher **Straight Arrow Publishers**
Category **Story Presentation**
Date **1986**

RED-HOT BLUES

FASHION BY LAURIE SCHECHTER

PHOTOGRAPHS BY STEVEN MEISEL

TWENTY-TWO YEAR OLD CUBAN BORN ACTOR AND MODEL **RICHARD ULACIA,** WHO STARRED IN PAUL MORRISSEY'S 1985 FILM *MIXED BLOOD* AND IS SLATED TO APPEAR IN *COLD IN COLOMBIA.* PLAYS HIS LATEST ROUGH BOY CHARACTER FOR *ROLLING STONE.* WEARING THE BEST JEANS AVAILABLE NOW TRIPLE BLEACHED, DOUBLE STONE WASHED, WORN TO DEATH DENIMS THAT SAVE YOU YEARS OF HARD WEAR. RICHARD PORTRAYS AN AT HOME KIND OF GUY FOR WHOM THE GREATEST COMFORT EQUALS THE GREATEST PLEASURE

471

471A

471B

233

471
Publication **Rolling Stone**
Art Director **Derek Ungless**
Designer **Raul Martinez**
Photographer **Steven Meisel**
Publisher **Straight Arrow Publishers**
Category **Story Presentation**
Date **1986**

THE
AFRICA
I CALL HOME

Searching through a politically tense region,
a photographer finds peace in the rhythms of the wild

Story and photographs by Anthony Bannister

TRAPPED under my car by a curious lioness that sits just five feet away, I find that I have only three exposures left in my camera—and more than 200 rolls of film locked in the car.

Deep in a swamp, I maneuver a boat all night to get close to a branchful of bee-eaters, only to watch them fly off into the inky jungle.

Or, even more disastrous, I travel hundreds of miles to photograph a wildebeest migration, and the last afternoon sun and wild desert flowers cause my brain to switch off. I take in the smells of dust and dying and flowers, and utterly forget to take pictures.

This, with all its inevitable frustrations, is part of the uncontrollable before I've found since the age of 10, when my family brought me to South Africa from England. They sent me to a rural boarding school in a part of the country that has the most astonishingly iridescent spiders. I was enraptured. Though I later became an electronics engineer, I took up wildlife photography full time as soon as I could get up the courage. The accompanying gallery is a result of my travels around the continent's incomparable southern region.

I like to spend a total of at least six months out of the year in the bush, getting around in a four-wheel drive vehi-

cle with a bed in the back. I pack it with food and water for two weeks—enough for me and, now and then, an adventurous sister and my 19-year-old son. In my search for wildlife, I'm helped by a great many people, both black and white, friends who spend their lives with the continent's most spectacular creatures.

The tragic thing is, the peace I've found in the bush cannot last. Even now, my boat includes areas that, like so much of Africa today, are torn by violence and heart by starvation. Occasionally, for instance, I try to shoot pictures in Angola and Mozambique—and have to avoid getting shot myself. And my own country of South Africa is struggling through the essential metamorphosis to a just society, though most of the violence is confined to the big cities. In my view, even without the politics and racial issues, the continent cannot survive its explosive population growth.

No matter what happens, though, they're going to have to bury me in Africa. I could never live permanently anywhere else. The patterns of the land and its creatures are etched too deeply in me. It's my home.

Since he became an award-winning filmmaker and photographer in 1974, Anthony Bannister has produced ten large-format books while contributing to this magazine and many others.

Standing with me (above) are friends Tiebe and Bo, two of the people I've met while spending some months out of each year in the wild. These !Kong bushmen, expert hunters, introduced my wife and me to the northern Kalahari Desert, sharing their campfires, meager water and vast knowledge of wildlife.

A Jackal's yelping alarm announced this leopard's presence (right). In Zimbabwe's Matopos National Park, I had about five seconds to snatch up my camera and shoot this portrait before the cat turned from me and fled.

42

472

These huddled little bee-eaters (left) roosted on a reed that overhung a waterway in Botswana's Okavango River Delta. I was fishing with friends in this rich wetland, whose clear waters spread out over the vast flats of the northern Kalahari. Having learned years ago that good wildlife shots turn up when you least expect them, I had a camera at the ready. Soon after, I resumed fishing and landed a good-sized bream.

Sunset throws a romantic light over the Namib Desert (above), where I first met my wife at a research station. But this belies the Namib's treacherous nature. Once, during a sandstorm, I set my bag down to take a picture. A moment later, it had disappeared, along with $20,000 worth of equipment. Having marked the spot with a tripod, I returned next day and searched for hours before finding the equipment under several inches of sand.

47

Frostbite was the last thing on my mind when a park warden showed me migrating wildebeest (right) in one of his aerial patrols over the Kalahari Desert. He even let me out the car door with no pocketknife. As we sped over the herd, my eyes teared up, and I could only aim the camera in the general direction and hope my frozen finger was releasing the shutter. The temperature on the ground that midwinter morning: just 12 degrees F.

When I saw this chameleon (above) crossing a hot road in South Africa's Kruger National Park, I stepped my car. The adaptable reptile was walking stiff-legged and on tiptoe to avoid the burning asphalt. Only when I focused the lens, however, did I notice the grasshopper riding piggyback, having discovered its own solution to crossing the road. After I stopped laughing, I found that my knees and elbows had been badly scorched.

44

472A

I was more frightened while photographing this herd (right) in South Africa's Addo Elephant National Park than at any other time in my life. Once heavily hunted, Addo elephants are notorious for their shyness and quick temper. Biologist Anthony Hall-Martin and I hid beside a little-known waterhole until a shadow fell across us. Ten feet away, the animals passed. One youngster came up and sniffed my tripod until his mother nudged him.

Sun-tumbled agate pebbles (above) lie along the Namib Desert's Skeleton Coast, named for the shipwrecks that litter some thousand miles of remote beaches. After dark, the eerie howls of scavenging jackals fill the night as a bone-chilling Atlantic fog creeps in. One night, a jackal stole my stones from under my camp bed. While following its tracks the next morning, I happened upon these delightful stones—but never did recover my shoes.

48

472C

Sensing danger, these red lechwes (right) take to the water of the Okavango River Delta. Most of the time, they calmly graze grass that stands in ankle-deep floodplains; but sometimes they gallop with a soaring, splashing gait. To get this shot, I chose a long meadow with water just five or six inches deep: enough to give the right effect as the red lechwes run. Then I concealed myself behind a large termite mound.

Each spring, wild flowers (above) burst through the gray gravel of South Africa's arid Atlantic Coast. This is part of the newly proclaimed Langebaan National Park, only an hour's drive north of Cape Town. Just offshore, a chain of islands hosts thousands of gannets and penguins.

Back cover: On South Africa's Malgas Island, where I captured the comical expression of this gannet, the awful stench of rotting fish permeated my equipment. But such discomforts are outweighed by the privilege of practicing my profession in some of the wildest places on Earth.

50

472D

234

472
Publication **International Wildlife**
Art Director **Dan Smith**
Designer **Dan Smith**
Photographer **Anthony Bannister**
Publisher **National Wildlife Federation**
Category **Story Presentation**
Date **May/June 1986**

The Incredible Egg

By Mark Wexler   Photographs by Frans Lanting

It is one of nature's greatest creations, a treasure men have risked their lives for; now, in Los Angeles, the world's largest collection of eggs is providing an invaluable tool for science

473

Natural Treasures

473B

"Many museums and universities have treated bird eggs like unwanted stepchildren."

473A

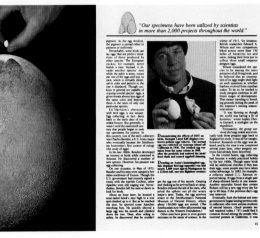

"Our specimens have been utilized by scientists in more than 2,000 projects throughout the world."

235

473C

473
Publication **National Wildlife**
Art Director **Dan Smith**
Designer **Dan Smith**
Photographer **Frans Lanting**
Publisher **National Wildlife Federation**
Category **Story Presentation**
Date **December 1986**

NOVEMBER 1986

Progressive Architecture

MOCA Moves In

The much-heralded first U.S. building by Arata Isozaki & Associates is a striking new home for a museum of contemporary art, as well as a focal point for the major urban redevelopment that paid for the museum, in an innovative use of public art funding.

The Museum of Contemporary Art, view from south

474

474A

JUNE 1986

Progressive Architecture

Rafael Moneo

With this article, P/A introduces to its readers Madrid architect Rafael Moneo, now Chairman of the Architecture Department at Harvard's Graduate School of Design. On the next pages, Moneo's recently completed National Museum of Roman Art in Merida, Spain, is shown. Following the museum is coverage of two earlier buildings by Moneo. Also included are comments from an interview of Moneo by P/A editors (p. 78).

236

475

475A

474
Publication **Progressive Architecture**
Art Director **Richelle J. Huff**
Designer **Samuel G. Shelton**
Photographer **Richard Bryant**
Publisher **Penton Publishing Co.**
Category **Story Presentation**
Date **November 1986**

475
Publication **Progressive Architecture**
Art Director **Richelle J. Huff**
Designer **Samuel G. Shelton**
Photographer **Luis Casals, Deide von Schaewen**
Publisher **Penton Publishing**
Category **Story Presentation**
Date **June 1986**

476

476A

476
Publication **Progressive Architecture**
Art Director **Richelle J. Huff**
Designer **Richelle J. Huff**
Photographer **Peter Aaron/ESTO**
Publisher **Penton Publishing Co.**
Category **Story Presentation**
Date **August 1986**

THE PARTINS:
THE NEXT GENERATION

PHOTOS BY GEORGE SKENE

Bo and the bull

Bo Vance, 13, grandson of Louis Partin, with one of his grandfather's registered show bulls. "A rabbit beaus 20," who weighs about as much as two average family car, but can be handled with ease by an experienced cowboy.

477

Easy riders

This is working cowboys and representatives of the fifth and fourth generation of Partins: Carlson Partin, 13; Dusty Colleran, 18, both grandsons of Louis Partin, 44; Sue Partin, 33; and Sarah's son, Mike Partin, 43.

On the fence

Ray F. Partin, 7; Bon Partin, 7; Ricky Booth, 8; and Brandy Vance, 10, all know how to ride horses before they began kindergarten. That's not unusual to this family, the children's parents, grandparents and great-grandparents did the same. But will this fifth generation of Partins go on to be cowboys? That remains to be seen, given family history, however, we'd bet on it.

At home on the range

Bo was both a native of the Australian outback, but Doug Partin, 34, was born and raised just south of Orlando. Doug, one of Sue Partin, played football as the University of Florida in the '70s, earned a degree in animal husbandry, then returned to the family ranch. He now manages a ranch near Kenansville that helps out on his father's ranch in his "spare" time.

477B

John boy

He's got two good reasons to chew tobacco: He's both a cowboy and a baseball player. John Partin, 23, represents what his grandmother, Mildred "Patsy" Partin, refers to as "our hope for the future of ranching." He attended Rollins College on a baseball scholarship, earned a degree in economics and has returned to work on the family ranch.

477A

238

477
Publication **Florida Magazine**
Art Director **Santa Choplin**
Designer **Santa Choplin, Bill Henderson**
Photographer **George Skeene**
Publisher **Sentinel Communications Co.**
Category **Story Presentation**
Date **November 23, 1986**

478

478A

478
Publication **The New York Times Magazine**
Art Director **Diana LaGuardia**
Designer **Kevin McPhee**
Photographer **Sebastiao Salgado**
Publisher **The New York Times**
Category **Story Presentation**
Date **September 7, 1986**

PORTRAIT
OF THE BRITISH

Dilapidated as it may be in other
ways, the author says, England still has
its full quotient of eccentrics.

By John Russell

Photographs by Neil Slavin.

479

479A

The 11th Duke of Devonshire and his
Duchess are manifestly 'the real
thing,' though no one could say they
dressed up to be photographed. It is
possible in England to dress up by
dressing down, but it's a good idea to
be a duke before you try it.

479B

240

479
Publication **The New York Times Magazine**
Art Director **Diana LaGuardia**
Designer **Audrey Razgaitis**
Photographer **Neil Slavin**
Publisher **The New York Times**
Category **Story Presentation**
Date **March 9, 1986**

The Struggle

Power and Politics In South Africa's Black Trade Unions

By Alan Cowell

Alan Cowell is chief of The New York Times bureau in Johannesburg.

On the 10th anniversary of the Soweto uprising, the white Government braces for a nationwide strike.

Africa's most modern economy depends on the black labor movement, legalized just seven years ago.

The black unions must strike a balance between gains in the workplace and long-term political goals.

480
Publication **The New York Times Magazine**
Art Director **Diana LaGuardia**
Designer **Diana LaGuardia**
Photographer **Susan O'Connor, Mark Peters, Abbas, Louise Gubb Venzago**
Publisher **The New York Times**
Category **Story Presentation**
Date **June 15, 1986**

JOB OF THE YEAR

BY MARILYN WEBB

The New Eighties Father is short on discipline and long on hugging and kissing and being a pal

PHOTOGRAPHS BY MARK HANAUER

481

Pictures of the Year

482

481A

242

482A

481B

482B

481
Publication **Us Magazine**
Art Director **Robert Priest**
Designer **Janet Waegel**
Photographer **Mark Hanaver**
Publisher **Us Magazine Co.**
Category **Story Presentation**
Date **June 16, 1986**

482
Publication **Sports Illustrated**
Art Director **Steven Hoffman**
Designer **Steven Hoffman**
Photographer **Various**
Publisher **Time, Inc.**
Category **Story Presentation**
Date **December 22, 1986**

244

245

LEGENDARY PRINTING

The Hennegan Company tradition of excellence began more than one hundred years ago, in 1886. We are proud of our long heritage of producing quality lithography for clients who expect only the best. Our rich tradition of creative collaboration with the world's finest designers, illustrators, and photographers has made Hennegan's "Showmanship in Printing" a unique standard for our clients to enjoy.

SHEET-FED

From the very beginning, Hennegan's superior capabilities in sheet-fed lithography created the basis for our world-wide reputation for excellence in printing. We do it with the ultimate in today's technology, from our new six-color, 40-inch Heidelbergs to our 60-inch multi-color capability and UV coating expertise. To this day, Hennegan stands unmatched among the highest quality printers anywhere.

WEB

Early in 1987, The Hennegan Company dedicated its first web offset press. Our new Baker Perkins G-14 Single Web 6-color press is the ultimate in heat-set web-offset printing machinery, configured and equipped to offer the highest in print quality to our customers. With its wide range of in-line folded products and electronically controlled press operation it provides the same fine quality for our customers that Hennegan has been delivering for over a century.

PRE-PRESS

At Hennegan, craftsmanship creates the difference between good printing and great lithography. And, using the sophisticated technology of Hennegan's pre-press, production, and finishing departments, talented craftsmen are consistently expanding the acknowledged standards of printing quality and performance.

We believe our legendary devotion to customer needs combined with equipment that is state-of-the-art for quality sheet-fed and web printing, will continue to underline Hennegan's commitment to the excellence demanded by our discerning clients.

Showmanship in Printing – Since 1886

311 Genesee Street, Cincinnati, Ohio 45202 513-621-7300